MW00745496

A CUP OF COMFORT®

for

Mothers

Stories that celebrate the women
who give us everything

Edited by
Colleen Sell

For my amazing mother, Jeannie Sell

Published by
World Publications Group, Inc.
140 Laurel Street
East Bridgewater, MA 02333
www.wrldpub.com

ISBN-10: 1-57215-744-5
ISBN-13: 978-1-57215-744-6
Printed and Bound in the United States of America.

10 9 8 7 6 5 4 3 2 1

This publication is designed to provide accurate and authoritative information with regard to the subject matter covered. It is sold with the
understanding that the publisher is not engaged in rendering legal,
accounting, or other professional advice. If legal advice or other expert
assistance is required, the services of a competent professional person
should be sought.
—From a *Declaration of Principles* jointly adopted by
a Committee of the American Bar Association and
a Committee of Publishers and Associations

Many of the designations used by manufacturers and sellers to distin-
guish their products are claimed as trademarks. Where those designations appear in this book and Adams Media was aware of a trademark
claim, the designations have been printed with initial capital letters.

Contents

Acknowledgments

My sincere thanks go to the folks at Adams Media for their professionalism, patience, good work, and good humor—especially the mighty triumvirate of Meredith O'Hayre, Paula Munier, and Karen Cooper.

And to the book's copyeditor, Gary Hamel.

And to the authors whose wonderful stories grace these pages.

But I am most thankful for my mother, Jeannie Sell, and for my children, Jennifer, Christine, and Mickey, my guiding light and the lights of my life in the incredible and infinite journey of motherhood.

Introduction

*"I looked on child rearing not only as a work
of love and duty but as a profession that was
fully as interesting and challenging as any hon-
orable profession in the world and one that
demanded the best I could bring to it."*
—Rose Kennedy

My mother is a poet. Unpublished. Unheralded. But a poet nonetheless. Not that she would ever admit it. Her poetry is not for public consumption. It is kept in a drawer—handwritten on sheets of unruled tablet paper, the kind used for real letter writing—with certain pieces read by a select few on rare occasions. Once in a blue moon, Mom will read one of her poems aloud to one of us kids (though I'm sure she's read or recited them all to my father). My mother has written a special poem about each of her six children; they are her masterpieces. If ever I doubted my mother's love for me or understanding of "who I really am" (and what child doesn't at some point in their young lives?), I could never again have such doubts after hearing her read, with tears glistening in her deep brown eyes, the poem she wrote about and for me.

I am a writer, but not a poet. Yet, when I think of my mother and of motherhood, I always think of poetry.

When I was in college and first read Robert Frost's "The Silken Tent," I thought immediately of my mother. No, it was more than a mere thought. I envisioned her, felt her. All these years later, the poem still has that effect on me. It is like a metaphor for my mother's style of mothering, for her firm but freeing presence in my life—her silken tent gently billowing over me in the "sunny summer breeze" and her "loosely bound . . . silken ties of love and thought," extending from a sturdy "central cedar post," growing "slightly taut" in the capricious winds of life.

I wonder which poem my three children would associate with my mothering style, with the imprint I've made on and the role I play in their lives. Free verse, no doubt. I suspect they'd each choose a different poem but that all three would have similarities.

Shortly after giving birth to my first child, Jennifer, I happened upon a poem in a popular women's magazine that struck my funny bone—and a chord with me. (I've long forgotten which magazine, the title of the poem, and its author.) At the time, I was very young, a girl really, newly out of the nest and flying about as well as a turkey, and taking my job as a new mommy extremely seriously. Naturally, as young and inexperienced women are wont to do, I sized up the closest example of motherhood to me: my mother's. And decided I was going to do many things differently. That is what the poem was about.

"When I was growing up, my mother did [this], so with Jennifer, I did [that]," the poem read, giving a litany of parental scenarios in which Jennifer's mom did the opposite of her own mom. The closing line read something like, "And in the end, Jennifer grew up to be just like my mother."

In some ways, I did mother differently than my mom did. But in many ways, I followed her example. In the end, Jennifer is a little like my mom, a little like me, and a whole lot her own original self. And both Jennifer and her sister Christie have approached motherhood in ways both similar to and different from mine. I'm certain my mother's brand of mothering was also influenced by her mother and her grandmother.

As it turns out, there are many ways to be a good mother. The important thing is to do your very best, to do it with love, and to enjoy it.

The personal true stories in *A Cup of Comfort*® *for Mothers* celebrate the joy of motherhood and honor this most challenging, fulfilling, and venerable profession.

—*Colleen Sell*

Heart Stories

The twins are two; Thomas is three and a half. And I am forty-two . . . today. We're celebrating my birthday at my parents' house because we've sold ours and set our furniture to sea. We're en route from central Canada to South Africa, where we will live for the next three years. Carl, my husband, is overseas right now, scouting rental properties.

So the birthday party is small, just my children and parents. We've had my favorite dinner, baked scallops, and we've gorged on homemade chocolate cake. It may be small, but the party is raucous. Chocolate propels young children sugar-sky high. For an hour, Thomas, Jon, and Alex have been chasing each other around the loop of my parents' first floor. We eventually corral them to open my presents.

Carl left behind a lovely writing journal and some restorative eye cream (truly), and my parents have promised to babysit while I buy myself some decent clothes. There's one final present and it's from Thomas. He and my father slipped out yesterday for a covert excursion to the Dollar Store. That's all I know—but they're both beaming now.

My father prefaces the unwrapping. "Thomas chose this all by himself," he says. "Didn't you, Thomas?"

"Yes. It's a heart," he blurts out.

"I didn't help him at all," my father emphasizes. "We walked through the aisles of the store until he found something to give to you."

The package is soft and about the size of a dinner plate. My mother must have wrapped it so neatly. I slowly take away the paper, smiling the silly smile of someone opening gifts. It is indeed a heart. A heart that could only have come from a Dollar Store. Strands of metallic red tinsel wind in magnificent loops and bows around a thin wire frame. It shines like a halo for a rather flamboyant St. Valentine.

"I bought that for you, Mommy," Thomas says as I squeeze him.

"It's beautiful, sweetie. I love it." And I do, more than any possible birthday gift.

Thomas squirms out of my arms and rallies the troops. With a final burst of cocoa-power, they're off. I thank my parents for the celebration as they move to tidy up. Within an hour, all three kids are scrubbed and sleeping and my parents have retired to their books and bed. The house is quiet—except for my tumbling thoughts.

I imagine Thomas roaming the aisles of the Dollar Store. He has one arm outstretched, his hand lightly fanning the shelves as he passes. His eyes are steady, taking in all the gaudy trinkets on the lower two shelves. He only looks higher when he stops. I've watched him do this; I can picture his actions clearly. Yet, I cannot envision my three-year-old, as self-absorbed as any preschooler, bypassing trucks, glitter-glue, lollipops, and maybe even trains to choose a heart. It's not something he wants for himself. He was, it seems, thinking of me.

How can I resist symbolism? The most obvious interpretation is love. Thomas, like a woozy teenager, has given me the heart as a token of his undying love. Many other metaphors are ripe for picking: trust, courage, patience, forgiveness. I revel in my wondrously empathic child.

And then I sober. These are late-night literary indulgences. I don't know why Thomas chose the heart, and I was too engulfed by my own thoughts to have asked him. I do know that three-year-olds aren't normally inclined toward empathy or metaphor. He was not sending a complex message. Maybe he liked the smoothness or shininess of the heart, or perhaps it reminded him of a bedtime story or a *Thomas the Tank Engine* episode.

Any larger story of the heart must be my own, and there are many ways to tell it.

Here's one.

It's the day before my forty-second birthday and I'm weary. The kids haven't slept—again. I slam down the stairs at just past five in the morning, Alex in one arm and Jon in the other. Thomas follows closely behind. We squish into the dark couch, and I close my eyes against another day. *I can't do this.*

My parents have heard us. My father gets up, while my mother rests a little longer. They're in their seventies, and we've been living at their house for over a month. If I'm weary, they are utterly decimated by the burden of three boisterous grandchildren and a daughter suffering—still—from postpartum depression.

"Why don't you go back to bed for a while?" my father offers, his gray hair in uncharacteristic spikes. "I'll look after the boys."

No. This is my job. I'll do it. Again and again. Day after day.

We've been up for hours when the winter sky lightens. Two thick coffees have left me agitated, and the boys are bored with the toys we brought from home. I have to get out, but it's December in rural Nova Scotia. There are no open parks, no story-time gatherings, no playgroups, no swimming pools, no friends, not even a clear driveway to ride a tricycle. There's the mall, and we've already been there—many times. I decide to take the kids for a walk in the snow.

I drag the basket of winter clothes from the hall closet. Three snowsuits, but only five mitts, four mismatched boots, and two hats. I begin the daily roundup of lost clothing. By the time I have six boots and three hats, Alex is hungry and Jon has filled his diaper. Thomas has forgotten about going outside and is half-heartedly rebuilding his train tracks.

Raisins for Alex, clean diaper for Jon. I then begin threading toddler limbs into puffy winter clothes. It's like weaving spaghetti, and the twins protest. Thomas, being older, is usually easier to dress, but he's having none of it today. In fact, he strips what little he is wearing and flees at the sight of his snowsuit. The twins, immobilized in their winter gear, are whining. I feel heat rise to my face and I set my teeth to an unnatural bite.

I could ask for help, but for the second time this morning, I won't. There's a side to depression—mine, at least—that's indulgent. Not intentional and delicious like, say, chocolate cake, more like wrenching a loose tooth; there's satisfaction in the pain. So I let myself slip to a familiar but lonely place. The fall is easy and I don't contemplate the formidable return. I just continue to run after Thomas, waving his snowsuit like a lasso.

He thinks it's hilarious, either my childish antics or that he's really, really aggravating his mother. In any case, he keeps it up until the heat in my face flashes to my brain, ignites, and shoots back through my entire body. I catch him. He's still laughing when I heave his naked body into an old wicker chair in the living room. Baby skin and wicker. He's not laughing anymore.

So . . .

When Thomas and my father go shopping the following day, he chooses a heart. A heart to remember the smoldering fire in my head and those sorry scratches down his back. A heart to suggest the mother I could be.

That's one heart story, but there are others.

There is, for instance, the story of a beautiful winter morning that I want my kids to touch. We haven't much else to do, and I'm weary to the point of tears. Still, the pale December light against a crowd of snowy firs is something this displaced urban family cannot miss.

It would be easier to flip on the television and let Bob the Builder do the work. It would be easier to crawl back to bed and let my parents take over. It would even be easier to let the kids grow bored and to ignore the whines, just for a moment. I'll do none of these things—but not because I'm a self-indulgent depressive.

I won't give in to television because TV is passive and dulling and eternally available. This snowy morning is fleeting. It yearns for the taste, crunch, and tumble of my children. I won't crawl back to bed, because I'm blessed with patient, dedicated parents and I will not take them for granted. And I won't let my kids wallow in boredom, because they are as bright and beautiful as the morning outside. I won't, in other words, use depression as an excuse to stop parenting.

In this story, I'm trying. For over three years, I've been trying to raise small children, battle depression, and move across the world—seamlessly. I'm tired. Super Nanny herself would be fatigued. I get frustrated, and sometimes, as when Thomas's fair skin met the crumbling wicker, I fail disastrously. In *this* story, however, I'm allowed mistakes.

So . . .

When Thomas and my father go shopping for my birthday, Thomas chooses a heart. A heart to thank me for the countless times I've tried. A heart to thank me for the mother I am.

A few weeks after my birthday, we leave my parents' house and move to Africa. Our furniture is still adrift, but Carl has rented a house and borrowed beds and kitchenware. The tinsel heart, transported with care, is our only decoration. I hang it from a stray cable in the living room. The kids call it "Mommy's Heart" and they show it to me everyday. Not that it needs pointing out. The heart would be hard to miss in any house, but against our empty white walls, it's almost riveting.

That's okay. I like to be reminded. Not of my mistakes, not of *that* mistake, but of the shifting stories we tell ourselves about ourselves. The events before my forty-second birthday can't be changed or denied. But just as the winter sun casts both brilliant light and deep shadows, the slant of our stories changes with time, and mood, and circumstance. We craft our truths, and there's power in remembering and retelling all shades of motherhood.

—Katherine Barrett

This story was first published in the fall 2008 issue of *Mom Writers Literary Magazine.*

Top Ten Reasons I Love Being a Mom

"Mom, listen to what I wrote for you," said my nine-year-old son, Jordan.

He smoothed a piece of paper and began to read from it. "The Top Ten Reasons Why I Love My Mom," he read in full Letterman style. "Number ten—Mom, you know you have to start with number ten because that saves the best for last, right?"

I nodded and he continued.

"Number ten: because you sometimes make my favorite dinner and you don't always make me finish my peas."

I smiled and he read number nine.

"Because you give really good backrubs." Jordan's eyes twinkled as he ran down his list.

"Number eight: because you don't make me kiss you in front of my friends."

I laughed and said, "You should want to kiss me!"

"Well, not when my friends are around," he said and then pointed at the paper in his hands. "Do you want to hear this or not?"

"Continue," I said with a the-floor-is-yours motion.

"Thank you," he said. "Number seven: because I always get an A when you help me with my homework."

I giggled and said, "Well, I should hope so. You're only in fourth grade."

"Mom, stop interrupting me," he groaned. "Okay, number six: because you cheer really, really loud when I score a goal in soccer."

"That's because I'm proud of you. Not because you scored, but just because you tried your best."

Jordan rolled his eyes. "All the grown-ups say that. Anyway, here's number five: because you listen to me read Goosebumps books and you don't even get scared."

I laughed but didn't say anything. I could tell Jordan was anxious to share the rest of the list with me.

"Number four: because you always laugh at my jokes."

I laughed again, just to prove his point.

"Number three," Jordan continued. "Because you usually close my bedroom door instead of making me clean my room." He looked at me solemnly and said, "I really, really appreciate that one, Mom."

I gave him my best Mom look and said, "Keep reading. I love your list."

"Okay, number two: because you listen to my prayers at bedtime and any problems I'm having at school." He shrugged and added, "I know they probably seem silly to you because you're a grown-up, but you still listen."

I smiled and hugged him. This list was so precious, and I could hardly wait to hear the number-one reason he loves me.

"Are you ready, Mom?" Jordan said. He did a drum roll on his thighs and announced, "And the number-one reason why I love you is . . . because you always have gum in your purse!"

I just have to say, "Ouch."

My son, whose birth lasted twenty hours and to whom I have given everything I have to give in the nine years since, loves me because I carry Juicy Fruit in my purse. Seriously, Juicy Fruit. He didn't write that I love him unconditionally. He didn't write that I make meeting his physical, emotional, and spiritual needs a top priority in my life. And he didn't write that I—oh, I don't know—gave him life. No, none of those reasons made the list. The number-one reason he loves me is that I carry chewing gum in my handbag.

I laughed, kissed his cheek, and thanked him for his clever list.

But the truth is, it bothered me a little bit. As a mother, I feel like I do a lot for my children. I cook their meals, I wash their clothes, and I clean up after them. Constantly. I make sacrifices on their behalf. I do without things so they can have what they want. But they don't see that. They don't see everything I do for them. And sometimes, it hurts. They appreciate me, but not for the reasons I want them to.

That night at bedtime I hugged Jordan and thanked him again for writing his top-ten list. I didn't want him to see that I wasn't completely thrilled with his number-one reason. After all, he was only nine years old. Maybe to him, carrying gum in my purse meant I should be expecting to get my Mother of the Year nod any time now. Either way, I decided to let it go. Just the fact that he wrote the list was beyond sweet.

"Did you like my list, Mom?" he asked. "Because I thought of one more, even though I'm out of numbers. This one is number zero: I love you because you're just the best mom ever and I don't think anyone could be as good at that as you are." He gave me the sweetest smile.

Tears gathered in my eyes as I gathered my little boy in my arms. He didn't love me because I'd endured a heinous episiotomy for him or because I haven't had a moment to myself since 1998. But he did love me. And that, in itself, is something to be grateful for.

—*Diane Stark*

Fair Division

My daughter won't read this until she's older, if she ever does. Right now, while I'm writing, she's snoozing away next to me on the couch. She is six years old, she's just lost her fifth tooth, and the number of her freckles is uncountably pretty.

When I'm done here, I'll carry her up to bed. Even though she's fast asleep, she'll hold on to my neck when I say so and I'll counter the weight of her sleeping body as I make my slow ascent up the stairs. In the morning, she'll say, "Let's get up now, Mom," and I'll say, "Five more minutes," and I'll wrap her satiny pajama'd body back inside my arms for one more dream.

The only problem is, this scenario isn't true. My daughter is not snoozing away next to me on the couch. She's tucked in bed at her dad's house downstate. In two more days, though, she'll really be here. I can already sense her weighting the cushions, can already feel the featherlock of hair that I'll smooth off her face. I can hear her chewing in her sleep. In two days, she'll be with me for a long weekend, but tonight it's just me, typing away the minutes until I can go get her.

I'll wake up alone tomorrow, but in two days, she and I will thread the lilac trees with a winter's worth of yarn scraps for the birds to use in their nests. We'll play Uno, and she'll say that when she grows up, she's going to be a horse doctor and we'll live together on a farm. She'll say she will buy me my own pony and we'll name her Lucy and feed her wild carrots. And then when I tuck her in, I'll read her some more of the latest book it's taking us months to get through. When I put it down and shut off the light, she'll close her eyes and I'll tell her stories about when I was pregnant. We'll imagine she is still there, inside me, her long legs stretching down my own and her arms threaded inside mine, reaching well past my elbows already. She'll laugh, but I'll wish it were somehow so, that she was still wrapped safe where nobody could claim she wasn't a part of me.

Or maybe this time I'll whisper to her the story of King Solomon.

I will tell her that long, long ago two women came to the king's court, one woman holding a baby's arms and the other pulling at his feet. Each said the child was hers.

Each claimed the other woman was lying. Solomon only had their words to figure out who was the real mom. So he took the baby from the women and laid him on the table. He held a sword over the child, and said that since he couldn't figure who was telling the truth, he would split the baby in two so each could have half of him. One woman said this was fair enough. The other stayed his hand; she'd rather the child be whole in the other woman's custody than that he be killed. And by this King Solomon knew who the true mother was, and he handed him over to her, all in one piece.

Now, I don't really buy that the first woman wanted to go home with half of a baby, but the point is, I'll tell my daughter, some people get caught up in numbers. They forget that numbers aren't real things but quantities of things. They're adjectives, really. Six, thirty-four, fifty-five—these are simply words that describe the value we place on a thing. We can't always make decisions based on numbers alone. If all that the first woman heard was half for you, half for me—if it were an orange being divided and not a child—then, sure, Solomon's judgment seems fair. But the other woman knew that this quotient was worth so much less than nothing.

That'll make sense to my daughter.

It's one of the things she gets from me, how good she is with numbers. Her blue eyes come from both me and her dad. The widow's peak that crowns her forehead—that's all his doing. But her round little knees and her fair skin and the way she is so calm and her ease with math—she shares those with me.

Just the other day on the phone, she told me she loved me to the moon and back a googol times. That's a really big number, she said. I told her I couldn't think of a bigger number than that: a one with a hundred zeroes marching behind. And really, in the moment, I couldn't. A googol plus one, she offered. A googol squared. And if she hadn't already been my girl, I would have fallen over myself in love with her right there.

They don't usually talk about people or happiness in math, but just like her googoled love, it's almost always about something more than the numbers. Like fair division, an odd subfield all about how to divide things up fairly. Not necessarily equally, which is easy, but in such a way that all the people involved are happy. Any good mom instinctively knows the rules of fair division. The classic example is splitting a cake into two so that both cake eaters are happy with their share. Mom gives the knife to one kid, who cuts the cake in half, and the other kid gets to pick which piece she wants. This means the cutter will try to divide the cake as evenly as possible so that she won't be stuck with the smaller piece her sister leaves on the plate. But really, who lets two children split and eat a whole cake? A cookie might be a better example; but face it, if a mom has one cookie and two children, she'll take it into the bathroom and eat it herself, just to avoid the situation altogether.

Two children and one mother, this makes sense. But when the situation is two parents and one child, and it's the child's life that needs splitting, that's where the whole idea of fair really breaks down. The problem is that a child is indivisible.

There's a recognition in fair division that monetary value is not the only value we place in things. When calculating a divorce settlement, for example, each person assigns value to what needs to be divided. How much could a couple's dog really be worth, on the market? Real estate and cars can be sold and the proceeds split in half, but what of her grandmother's wedding band, his dad's canoe? We decide what we want most and we say so.

She asked me, early on, "Why did you leave me with Dad?"

She should know that it's not because he and I made a list of all our assets and ranked them by importance and that my thinking chair or my library desk (the only furniture in our whole big house I took with me) were listed higher than her. I didn't leave with so many things I still wanted: my grandma's piano, at least one of the Scrabbles, the big blue mixing bowl. I wanted her bad. I still do.

But I forgot to say so loud enough. Fair division calculators don't take into account when people are scared. Or maybe what I wanted most was to leave her dad and saying that very hard thing left me without the strength to say the other things that needed articulating.

With her dad, she has a parent with a real job, with health insurance; she has a step-parent. She wouldn't have any of that with me, although she knows we'd work it out. She's said to me, "I wish I lived with you, and my dad only got one minute with me every year." I know she was exaggerating, but that's about how fair our visitation schedule seems. Only I am the one who gets the sixty seconds of her time for us to imagine her living with me.

I want to tell her, "Know that I didn't think I would be leaving you."

I thought her dad and I agreed about what was fair. Or I simply didn't believe he could leave with her to a new job seven hours south of here. When I trace back what I did wrong, I am led to numbers and words: long, mean documents that measure and partition time and physical custody. But worse is what these things have come to mean: that I have to keep her bedroom door closed when she is away. That I have not taken a picture of her in two years because any album would reveal the white spaces between photographs.

There's no fair division in the custody of a little girl. Whichever parent doesn't get to tuck her in at night loses. Every time her father and I meet midway and I pick her up, the world is an hourglass just turned over. When I drop her off, the weight of the empty seat next to me could nearly tip the car on its side.

When I tell her dad I need more time with her, he says, "I do lots to keep her connected to you. I always mention how good her mother is with numbers."

And I say, "I said I need more time with her."

He says, "I picked this elementary school because it has been part of a pilot program in math."

I say, "Listen."

I want to talk about time and he speaks to me of numbers. I'm talking about our daughter and he's talking about her report card.

No matter how specific, how official, the words and numbers, they all depend on us to interpret them with care. That's part of the reason I've never told her about King Solomon; it's too likely she'll think that in that story she is the baby and I am the righteous real mother, when that's not what I mean. Because even though the child's real mother got to take him home in the end, she was wrong. She really should have said the words out loud: Do not cut my baby in half. She's lucky it worked out for them both, but it might not have. It doesn't always.

And that's why I haven't been able to write this before tonight, on a day when I've met with a lawyer, a young man who will help me not be scared to say the right things out loud in a language the people who draw up these documents understand. Because I want to apologize to her. But more, I want to recalculate how we talk about everything.

So, sure, baby, I'll tell her next time she's with me, love your numbers. But remember to love more what's real behind the numbers. Love the dates on the calendar that are marked Mom, and love the inches sketched in pencil on the wall where I trace you growing, and love the digital radio frequencies that light up the dash as we sing our way north across the Mackinac Bridge to our house up here and then back again, toward your dad. When the hours that you and I need to pass before we're together are too many, sweet girl, imagine the Fourth of July. Think of us wrapped in a blanket, heads tilted up toward the sky patterned with color. When time moves too slowly or too quickly, stop counting the minutes and miles. Tell me that story about the pony named Lucy, in the years down the road when the division of your time will be calculated by you.

—*Jennifer A. Howard*

This story was first published in LiteraryMama.com.

The Tiring, Exhausting, Patience-Testing, Very Long Day

One of my favorite childhood books was *Alexander and the Terrible, Horrible, No Good, Very Bad Day*, by Judith Viorst. It is a story about a little boy who is having one of those days when absolutely, positively nothing seems to go his way.

My children were about three and five years old when I rediscovered the book and read it to them. To my surprise, my children did not take to *Alexander* as I had anticipated. In fact, their response was lukewarm, at best. Was it because the book was still a bit "old" for them? Was it too long? Was it because the pictures were in black and white? Nope. Those weren't the problems. The real reason the story didn't jibe with my kids is that they simply could not relate to having a bad day. Why, they didn't even know what a bad day was! I mean, really, who was I kidding here? Their days are full of fun and wonder and excitement made possible by two doting parents attending to their every wish and need!

I, on the other hand, really felt for Alexander and reconnected with him the first time I read the book to my children. I truly understood, even better than when I was a kid, what Alexander was going through. I could relate all too well to what it was like to have a terrible, horrible, no good, very bad day when nothing went your way . . . nothing at all, no matter how hard you tried, how efficient or organized you thought you were, or how many lists you made. Some days just don't warrant getting out of bed. Some days just last forever. Some days just suck every ounce of strength, energy, and dignity right out of your very soul. A day like this . . .

My two preschoolers march into my bedroom demanding to go to the park [Charlotte], play outside in the rain [Andrew], build a tree house [Andrew], bake double chocolate chip cookies with sprinkles on top [Charlotte], paint pictures, dig up the potatoes in the garden [Charlotte], have a snowball fight with last year's snowballs still stored in the deep freezer [Andrew], and go swimming [ah, consensus]. Of course, Andrew wants to go to the pool with the rope swing and Charlotte wants to go to the pool with the diving boards.

I open one eye, roll over in bed, and look at the clock. It is 5:39 in the morning. In that moment, I know right then and there, it is going to be a dreadful, exhausting, patience-testing, very long day.

For breakfast, Charlotte wants two poached eggs on toast with no butter, orange juice in a plastic cup, and a yellow vitamin. Andrew wants one scrambled egg with ketchup, toast with butter cut into squares (not triangles), apple juice in a glass, and a blue vitamin. As it would be, the egg carton is empty, there are only green vitamins left, and I give Andrew milk instead of juice.

"I didn't order milk, I ordered juice," Andrew informs me.

I inform him that I will just take them both to a restaurant tomorrow.

Andrew dresses himself in his favorite Pokémon outfit, which he has worn for the last six days. It is not too disgusting, yet—it only has a bit of mustard and soy sauce on the front and some blue paint on one sleeve.

Charlotte also dresses herself . . . in a dress two sizes too big for her that drags on the floor. She trips and falls. So I pick her up and tell her I love her.

"I love Mr. Cowie." Mr. Cowie is our neighbor.

I sigh, knowing it is going to be a dreadful, exhausting, patience-testing, very long day.

In the garden, Andrew sneaks off to eat raspberries and then decides to dig a big hole to "catch" all the rain and snow, while Charlotte hunts for lady-bugs. Alas, it is Andrew who finds a ladybug first, which is cause for a huge temper tantrum. Fortunately, I find a ladybug for Charlotte. Unfortunately, she doesn't want it because the ladybug is not yellow. I tell her that ladybugs don't come in yellow, which serves only to make her even madder.

"I am going to hunt for worms!" she declares defiantly.

It is very quiet. It is too quiet, and then I hear it—coughing and sputtering. And then I see it—dirt and worm slime all over Charlotte's mouth. Charlotte is kissing the worms she found, one by one. Charlotte says the worms love her. She says she loves the worms. I calmly explain to her that worms prefer to have kisses blown to them. Then I shake my head. It is a dreadful, exhausting, patience-testing, very long day.

As we get ready to go grocery shopping, Andrew decides he must wear his rubber fireman boots, his fireman slicker, and his fire chief hat. Charlotte wants to change into her yellow shirt and yellow shorts, but she doesn't have yellow shorts. I tell her I will buy her some yellow shorts tomorrow.

On the way to the store Andrew counts twenty-seven fire hydrants and Charlotte counts eleven yellow cars. Andrew complains that Charlotte is looking out his side of the car and Charlotte complains that all the cars are on Andrew's side. She is mad because the stoplight turned green and not yellow. She wants her window up because she is cold, and Andrew wants his down because he is hot. He kicks off his rubber boots, and Charlotte starts crying because she doesn't have any rubber boots. I tell Charlotte I will buy her yellow shorts *and* rubber boots tomorrow. Andrew wants to know what I am going to buy him. I am thinking that tomorrow will also be a dreadful, exhausting, patience-testing, very long day.

Once we are at the store, I can't find my grocery list. Charlotte wants to buy everything and anything yellow and starts filling up the cart with bananas, grapefruit, and lemons. While I search for my list, I hear Andrew informing other customers what to do in case of a fire. I really don't know if I will make it until tomorrow.

We're finally home. Once again, it is quiet. It is very quiet. It is too quiet, and I can't find Andrew and Charlotte. Then I hear a giggle from behind the couch and see that Andrew has taken a bottle of balsamic vinegar from the grocery bags. He is pouring shots of it in Charlotte's plastic cups for himself and his sister. They look up with great big smiles and balsamic vinegar moustaches. Their clothes are a mess and the carpet is a mess and the couch is a mess.

"I'll clean it up tomorrow," I say, assuming I last through this dreadful, exhausting, patience-testing, very long day.

At bath time, Andrew is upset that Charlotte hops into the tub before he does and Charlotte is upset that Andrew gets to sit in the front. Andrew wants bubble bath, and Charlotte wants yellow bath beads, but there are only purple ones left. They both don't want their hair washed unless I will make dinosaur horns with the shampoo. Charlotte wants three horns so she can be triceratops, and Andrew wants to be tyrannosaurus Rex.

I tell them I will be right back. I tell them I will be gone for just a couple of seconds. I tell them I am just going to get their pajamas. By the time I return, there is water all over the floor, tyrannosaurus Rex has smashed triceratops's three horns, and triceratops has soap in her eyes and is screaming loudly. I shake my head and say that it has been a dreadful, exhausting, patience-testing, very long day.

At bedtime, Andrew wants to sleep in his one-piece pajamas, not his two-piece pajamas. He wants socks on his feet *and* socks on his hands *and* his blue winter hat on his head *and* a sweater. He also wants his teddy bear, Smoky, *and* Smoky's family. There are eleven bears in Smoky's family. But then he tells me he doesn't want to sleep with Smoky after all, because Smoky is a chatterbox and keeps him awake at night. I take Smoky and Smoky's family out of the bedroom.

Charlotte wants to sleep in her yellow pajamas, which are dirty—not the purple pajamas and not the red pajamas with the little red hearts, the yellow ones and only the yellow ones. So I dig to the bottom of the dirty clothes pile and actually find them. They are too disgusting for words, but on they go. Then I have to find Charlotte's baby lamb, the mommy lamb, the special blanket that Nana made, and seven books (exactly).

I finally relax on the couch only to look up five seconds later to see Andrew *and* Charlotte standing there.

"We have something important to tell you," Andrew says.

He states that he needs a drink of water, his tummy is hungry, and he hears a noise in his room.

Charlotte can't find her baby lamb, she doesn't want any books in her room, and she wants to sleep in her party shoes.

My dreadful, exhausting, patience-testing, very long day is still not over.

Finally, all is quiet, so I open the door to their bedroom and silently tiptoe across the room. I look down at their angelic little faces, so perfect, so peaceful, so beautiful.

I think what a wonderful, pleasant, terrific, very good day it has been. I can hardly wait until tomorrow.

—Tessa Graham

My Mother's Hands

Once, perhaps ten years ago, I was having dinner with a very good friend, JoAnne Pierce. JoAnne and I taught together for many years, and from the first time we met, we "clicked." She's ten years older than I; our interests are very different, as are our beliefs and faith. But we understand each other, and it's one of life's joys to have such a soul in one's life. JoAnne is one of my ya-yas, sure 'nuff. And that night, as women have done throughout the ages, we were discussing aging.

"It's my hair," I wailed, running my hands through it ruefully. Soon as I hit thirty, the gray started creeping in. "Lord only knows what's actually growing under all that Miss Clairol."

"Nah," she said, running her fingers through her own gorgeous blond hair, which, disgustingly, still, to this day, has no gray in it. "I'll tell you how you know. One day you'll look down while you're washing dishes or cleaning something, and you'll see your mother's hands—wrinkled, with age spots, nails all brittle and split. That's when you'll really know."

I looked down at my hands, my wonderful BC (before children) hands, and couldn't imagine them on my mother. The nails were long and manicured; the skin still soft and unblemished. The hands of a young thirty-something, sans kids.

I remember my mother's hands. Those hands, right beside mine in a pan full of beans . . .

"Here now, watch Mama. Take the butterbean in your left hand and peel it open with the right. Now, just run your thumb down and slide the beans right out into the pan. No, no, don't pick each one out. Just slide your thumb down. Yes, we will get them all shelled, and no, it won't take forever. This is the easy work, child, sitting here in the shade. Want Mama to tell you a story while we work?"

Those hands, reaching out to grab me as I ran crying into the kitchen . . .

"Come here, honey. Aw, you skinned it up bad. Come here, get on Mama's lap, sugar pie. Hold Mama's hand tight, I'm gonna just clean it up with a soft washrag and some soap. Hold Mama's hand tight now. I'm so sorry, baby. Mama will make it better."

Those hands, reaching for her Bible, flipping through and finding her verse in record time . . .

"Now, the two of you just look right here. Right here: what's that say? That's right, 'Be ye kind.' 'Be ye kind' that's what Jesus wants you to do. You think it's kind to tease your little sister, Moses Archie? Connie, you think it's kind to come runnin' tattling on your own brother? Be ye kind. It's one of the most important things to do in life. Always be kind, children. Not just to each other, to everybody, you hear?"

Those hands, *tap tap tapping* on an old-fashioned adding machine, reaching up to pull down the handle with a *chi-ching!* every so often . . .

"You got to keep track of every penny you own, child. You double-check your bank statement every month, you hear? Don't never take for granted that they got it right. Be careful who you trust with your money, girl. You'll work too hard for it not to keep good track of what you make."

Those hands, reaching up to wipe a bead of sweat off her brow, knife in hand . . .

"Here, now, you take this knife—careful, now— and hold the ear of corn just like this. Now, just run the knife down, cutting off the kernels. Be careful! Your daddy sharpened every one of these knives last night; they'll cut your hand clean off if you're not careful. That's right, now turn the ear and cut another row. Yes, Lord, child, corn is a pile of work, but it's so good. Be so good this winter to have fresh corn froze, won't it? We so lucky to have such good food."

Those hands, reaching up to pull off two bands of gold, twisting and turning them, finally getting them off and handing them to her daughter . . .

"No, no, go on and take them now. Lord, my old arthritis is so bad, I can't hardly get them on and off. Want you to have them. Wear them, too. Don't want these rings shut up somewhere in a box. Go ahead, put them on; take them on home with you when you go. I don't need any rings anymore to tell me I'm married to your daddy. Been bonded to him forty-three years now. Been happy, too. You go on and take them. Hope you find someone who'll be as good to you as your daddy's been to me."

Those hands, slowly, slowly trying to lift a spoonful of applesauce to her lips . . .

"Well, I just don't think I can get it down. Heavens, that old chemotherapy makes you feel awful, that's what. Awful. Ah, me, well, if I can't get down a spoonful, I'll try half a spoonful, that's what. You got to keep fighting, child. Can't let nothing, not cancer, not hard times, nothing, keep you from fighting."

And the applesauce disappeared, slowly, painfully, one-half spoonful at a time.

Those hands, groping feverishly along the bed-clothes . . .

"I'm sorry, I'm so sorry. Hate to trouble folks. Hate that you have to take so much time to take care of me. It's not right; I never wanted to be a bother to no one. But it hurts so bad. So bad. I'm so sorry."

And I held the hands—held Mama's hands tight—until the morphine blessedly kicked in again.

I look down now at my own hands, ten years and two children later. The nails are split; that one finger is crooked from where I jammed it a few years back; and the twinges and slightly swollen knuckles tell me Miss Ida's arthritis lives again. I see my mother's hands. Not really, though. What I actually see is a pale imitation, something like a dutifully completed paint-by-number copy of a masterpiece created by da Vinci or Monet. I clasp them together and pray sincerely, "Oh, dear Lord, please, please give me my mother's hands."

—Connie Ellison

Butterfly

She peeks at me as she squats under a rack of women's blouses, mostly hidden from view. I smile at her tiny face and the dirt smudge across her cheek. Her eyes dance with playfulness as she reaches out and grabs at her mother's legs.

I am sitting in a faux velvet chair outside the dressing rooms, the sentry, while my daughter tries on evening gowns. We are shopping for her prom, only a month away. At eighteen, she is finishing her senior year of high school with one foot planted firmly in our home and the other already out the door. In the fall, she will go to college and leave home, leave me. I struggle with her parting and can't believe the time will come so soon.

It's as though I looked away, and now she's grown.

I glance back at the little girl. She is sitting, her legs splayed out in front of her. She has scooted farther under the rack, yet I have a better view of her now. Her blonde hair is held back with purple butterfly barrettes, or maybe they are bows. I wonder if her mother let her pick them out herself, as I often did with my daughter, while waiting patiently with her hairbrush.

I wave my fingers at her. She stares. I exaggerate a pouty face, sticking out my bottom lip. She hesitates, and then smiles, the corners of her mouth turning up toward the dirt smudge.

I wiggle my fingers again, using both hands this time. She looks around until her eyes pause with comfort on her mother. Then she looks back at me and mimics my wave. Her fingers are tiny, her wave barely visible amid the hanging fabrics above her.

The dressing room door creaks and I turn.

"Mom, will you hand me the green one?" my daughter asks.

I take the dress from my lap and pass it through the crack of the door.

Settling back in my chair, I look to the rack of blouses. The little girl sits with her elbows resting on her bent knees, her chin in her hands, staring at me. Sighing, I put my elbows on my knees and rest my chin in my hands. She giggles and folds her arms over her chest. I do the same. She crosses her ankles, and I cross mine. I pat the top of my head; she pats hers.

I laugh as I remember playing pat-a-cake with my daughter, her soft ringlets bouncing with each clap. I remember her standing on a chair at the kitchen table, covered in frosting as we made Christmas cookies. And when she would fall asleep on the couch, I remember the way her body felt, curled against mine.

"Mom?"

I turn toward the voice, and my daughter emerges, dazzling in emerald satin. She twirls, turning like a ballerina, shimmering in color. She is tall, with long legs and a woman's figure, unlike the little girl I knew for so long. Her blonde hair settles softly around her shoulders as she strikes a model's pose. Tears spring to my eyes.

"Mom, are you crying?" she asks, rolling her eyes. She leans over, the satin whispering, and hugs me. "You're so emotional." She kisses the top of my head as I wrap my arms around her, careful to keep my tears away from the expensive fabric.

"I'm not crying," I say. "These lights are just bothering my contacts."

I blink, and we laugh at my weak excuse.

She steps away and returns to the mirror.

"What do you think?" she asks, turning front to back.

I swallow as memories of her eighteen years flash through my thoughts, blurring the image of this beautiful young woman standing in front of me.

"I think you are amazing," I whisper.

We pause with each other, then *ooh* and *ahh* over the dress as we talk about the price and carefully check the material for flaws. After we settle on this being the one, she disappears back into the changing room.

I take a tissue from my purse and dab at my tears. With a start, I remember the little girl.

Turning to the clothes rack, I look for her. My eyes search for her blonde hair and beautiful hazel eyes. I bend over and look under the racks of clothes. Kneeling, I find a butterfly barrette.

It's as though I looked away, and now she's gone.

—*Tricia L. McDonald*

This story was first published in the summer 2007 issue of *Mom Writer's Literary Magazine*.

On Sons, at Four

My four-year-old boys love me like prepubescents experiencing their first crushes: wild, unadulterated, obsessive love, so fierce and fantastical it's almost embarrassing.

Both sons are caught in a full-on Oedipus complex, I know, I know. But do the boys have to be so starkly obvious about their feelings for me? After all, Freud's theories always seemed a bunch of patriarchal hooey, but I wonder, now, if my boys have his *Complete Works* tucked beneath their tractor-themed pillows, reminding them to fall in love with their mother.

These days, I receive countless marriage proposals from each. Something like: "I wish I married you before Daddy did." Daddy, of course, is the great interloper, the man who sleeps next to me most nights.

Or I should say, most of the night. Because my boys cannot fall asleep in the same room, they take turns going to sleep in "Mama's bed"—called this, even though it is clearly not mine alone. Each night, minutes before bedtime, the duel for Mama's bed ensues: "Is it my turn Mama's bed?" "He had Mama's bed last night." "I'm sure it's my turn Mama's bed." Once proper order is established, the winner runs off to my bedroom, triumphant; the loser slumps deject-edly to his room.

In Mama's bed (the name itself seems freighted with unwanted metaphor), I read a book while the victorious son gazes at me adoringly, his mama-princess, who enchants even while turning pages. Despite having a king-sized bed, each son chooses to fall asleep pressed against me, holding my hand. Later, their dad peels them from me, putting them in their own bed, their blissful turn with Mommy disappointingly over.

Freud, I think, would have a heyday with the symbolism of my husband's nightly intervention in the mama-bed drama.

Yet, the drama continues—for during the day, my boys fight over who I should hold and who gets to sit behind me in the car (if I drive, one son is happy; if my husband drives and I sit in the front seat, I've pleased the other son). They practice long, slow kisses, coming to me with lips puckered and eyes shut, much like that other guy who lives in our house. At dinner, they push their chairs suffocatingly close to mine, so that three of us sit tight on one side of the table. My husband sits alone on the other side.

The boys are true romantics, having learned—perhaps from SpongeBob, most definitely not from my husband—that women can be wooed with chocolate and flowers. When they receive chocolate, they always share, ceremoniously handing me a small piece squeezed in their sticky fingers, then waiting for acknowledgment of their great gift. Never mind that I had given them the chocolate to begin with.

Our yard has also been plucked free of dandelions, as the boys pick the weeds one by one, walking back and forth across the yard to deliver their presents, then insisting I display them in cups of water. For a short while, they also yanked my roses from their stems, bringing me buds mangled by their efforts. While I appreciated the sacrifice of pricked fingers, I stopped the practice so that my rose bushes might survive the summer.

It's nice, in a way, this Mama adoration; Freud be damned. After all, I haven't received this kind of elaborate romantic attention since my husband first pursued me a decade ago, not with chocolate or flowers, but with long romantic letters and weekend getaways to the coast. And while my husband continues to charm me, I appreciate the rush of young love and the sense that, at least to two little boys, I am the most extraordinary creature in the world.

Still, Freud promises this loving attention will soon depart and that, at five, they will no longer find me the goddess I now seem. If they are consulting the books stashed under their pillows, both boys will learn they need to identify with their father rather than to be in love with me.

And so I feel a small sadness that my sons' fifth birthday is looming. Hopefully, they can learn new ways to express their love to me. Picking up their socks would be a good place to start.

—*Melanie Springer Mock*

This story was first published on mamazine.com.

Just a Mom

Standing in front of the mirror, I square my shoulders, suck in my gut, and hold my chin up as proudly as any Marine's. Looking solidly back at my reflection, inhaling deeply, I pause a moment to get centered, grounded, and ready to practice for . . . the dinner party. Poise and attitude are required to answer the inevitable question. Stamina too, as it's the one most often asked and yet the one most likely to perplex people when I answer it.

I level my eyes and meet my own gaze in the mirror. "So," I say, in a deep baritone voice not my own. "What do you do?"

Pregnant pause.

"I AM A MOTHER!"

Oops. That sounded a bit too forced. I try again.

"Oh, I'm just a mom," I counter my image in the mirror with a shrug.

41

That was much too apologetic. That won't do at all. Again!

"I'm a mama, *madre*, domestic goddess, mother of two/stepmother of two. I'm the maker of men. Think Venus of Willendorf. I'm Gaia incarnate."

That was, perhaps, a bit over the top.

I throw up my arms and put on some lipstick.

It's not the question that throws me off so much as it is people's reactions to the notion that being a mother does not a job description make.

The worst reaction is the glazed eyes that turn downward, confused, as if they'd just learned I have a terminal illness.

My maternal response to the "What do you do?" question somehow completely manages to dam the flow of some conversations before they've ever begun. "Oh! You're a mother? Excuse me while I go freshen my martini and talk to the dentist over there."

Inevitably, I'll also get the arched eyebrows and piercing eyes. What could they be thinking in the ten seconds before they formulate a reply? "Full-time? How can that be financially possible in this day and age?" "How old are your children?" "Aren't you bored? What do you *do* all day?" I've heard it all.

Sometimes, I get the sage nod and sincere eyes and the slightly patronizing, "That's the hardest job in the world" reply, followed by a pat on the shoulder. No one would say that to a rocket scientist or a neurosurgeon, both general benchmarks for "hard" jobs—which, by the way, are compensated accordingly.

All the varied reactions sometimes make me want to stay home and just make macaroni and cheese for the masses. But what kind of challenge is that? I have to test my mettle at times and flex my ability to meet this call to honor creatively.

I have a friend who was an "at-home" mom for many years. I asked her how she handled the inevitable party question of "What do you do?"—or, if people already know your profession as a full-time mom, their careful probing of, "So what are you doing these days?" She knew exactly what I was talking about.

"One time," she said wryly, "I just said I'm letting my hair grow." Completely deadpan. She's very original.

Something happened in our culture between *Leave It to Beaver* and *The Mary Tyler Moore Show* that left being "just a mom" a socially awkward conundrum in our society. "What you do?" seems to be the all-consuming, burning question. And the answer had better be good enough.

Some women would never, ever want to be "just a mom," and that's totally okay with me. The truth is, technically, I've never been "just" a mom either; I've always been some combination of at-home mom and working mom. That's the way it is with many, if not most, mothers I know. We go through a sort of revolving door between work/motherhood, work/motherhood, work/motherhood. What bothers me is how conflicted many moms are despite which role is taking up the majority of our time. I've heard working mothers anguish over how much time their kids are spending at daycare. In the same circle, I might hear an at-home mom fret over not bringing in some much-needed money for school shoes or diapers. We never seem to be doing enough for ourselves, our families, or dinner party attendees.

I've never bought into the media-created "mommy wars," at all. There is a bond, a true understanding, between most mothers. Even a mother of only one child has done enough time with no-sleep nights, nipple drip guards, teething, and the sheer joy of witnessing Baby's first real smile to have respect for one of her own. Mothers quietly acknowledge motherhood as a noble occupation with nonexistent financial incentives. Most moms just "get it" and leave you alone, although admittedly some are more curious about how you put it all together than others.

My path has never been a straightforward one. Being a mom, is, in fact, a path that can lead in a thousand directions without ever really "getting" anywhere. It's a Zen path all its own.

I was nine months pregnant with my second child when I graduated from college. I had a sneaky suspicion that if I didn't push on through (to graduation), it might never happen. So, during that time, I wasn't only a mom, I was also a student. Then came the heavy-duty "at-home mom" years. Truly, I ran around chasing two wild boys all day long. But, even then, I took on strange odd jobs like "official pie and cornbread baker" for a local restaurant, which involved only a few hours a week, but it was enough to pay the babysitter for the occasional movie night out. There were stints as a fragrance model, crafter of pillows and blankets, secretary, temp worker, and even a few years during which I was a bookkeeper—a part-time bookkeeper. It was only a ten-hour-a-week job, but having it made going to parties a whole lot easier. I could say to the inevitable "What do you do?" question that I was a bookkeeper at a record store! Oh, wow, everyone wanted to talk with me then! Little did they know that 99 percent of my life was spent listening to Super Mario Brothers Nintendo or Disney soundtracks at home and not jazz or indie rock at the store. When my kids got a little older, I even had my own home-based business that did well for quite a few years.

Whether my for-pay work has been performed inside or outside the home, its main purpose has always been to support my real job: raising my kids.

Becoming a mom was my choice, and I love it and have absolutely no regrets. The attendees of dinner parties and our society at large need to take into account all the work that moms do. I don't just mean raising kids, including bathing, feeding, and clothing. There's also taking care of sick kids and taking them to medical and dental appointments. And chauffeuring them to friends' houses, outings, lessons, sports, and other activities. And crisis counseling with teens, crisis counseling other parents of teens, and sometimes the teachers of teens. And endless scheduling, chaperoning, volunteering, and shopping for school clothes, sporting equipment, birthdays, holidays, school supplies, school dances and parties. And helping with homework. And practicing music, dance, gymnastics, scouting, sports, or whatever your kids are involved with. And the phone tree, and play dates, and PTA meetings. And let's not forget filling out reams of paperwork, from preschool through college and into the kids' resume-writing years. Overtime, of course, includes sleepovers and early morning runs for donuts. Being a mom entails all this work and more without a paycheck, medical or 401k benefits, paid vacation, or other societal validations.

Being a mom is a hard job, an important job, and one that can be incredibly rewarding. At least it is to me and to the millions of other mothers out here, both "at-home" and "working outside the home," who take the job seriously. And love it. Even if we don't always get the recognition and respect we would appreciate at dinner parties.

So, tonight, facing my reflection in the mirror, I see a woman in between jobs again. My oldest son is moving out soon, and my step-sons are pelting the bathroom door with Nerf darts. Resolved to hold my head high at the party, I turn to leave and almost trip over my heels on a towel and boys' sneakers left on the bathroom floor. I'm still caught in that revolving door of work/motherhood, work/motherhood, work/motherhood. The funny thing is, I don't care if it ever stops spinning. I'm so happy to be a mom.

Maybe at the party when I'm asked the inevitable question, I'll just say I'm a door keeper at Chez Mama and see what kind of lively dialogue that sparks.

—*Elizabeth King Gerlach*

A Whisper

As I tuck my daughter in, I speak in Chinese. The last story has been read and it is bedtime.

"*Wo ai ni*, Jade" I say.

She giggles. "What it means?" my three-year-old daughter asks, enjoying her reprieve from sleep time.

"When a person is really important in your life, you tell them how much you care about them by saying, '*Wo ai ni*.' That is Chinese for 'I love you.'"

"Like Mama say to Daddy?"

"Yes, sweetie, Mama and Daddy love each other, so we tell each other, sometimes in English and sometimes in Chinese. The important thing is that we tell each other how we feel."

"Wannie, Mama!" Jade proclaims, as if she has just made a great discovery.

"*Wo ai ni*, baby. It's time to go to sleep now. I'll see you in the morning," I say with a kiss on her soft forehead.

"Like Mama sing in China?" she asks, as I am halfway out the door. She is obviously trying to delay the inevitable.

"What, sweetheart?"

"Like Mama sing to Baby Jade the first time."

"Oh, you mean when we first met?"

I had forgotten about my improvised song at the Civil Affairs Office in Changsha when my husband and I had first met Jade. She was almost two years old at the time, and she was the oldest and most vocal child in a room filled with other adoptive families meeting their babies for the first time. The moment she saw our faces and realized who we were, she completely melted down, vehemently protesting the proceedings. We held her, offered her toys and candy, but nothing calmed her. Finally, Kevin suggested that I sing to her. I was a trained opera singer, but unfortunately, did not know any children's Chinese songs. So, managing to improvise a believable Eastern melody, I sang the first words that came to my mind: "*Mama ai ni. Mama, Mama ai ni,*" which translates to "Mama loves you. Mama, Mama loves you." It worked like a charm, and Jade quieted immediately.

"Sing again, Mama, pleeeeese?" she begs, more to keep me in the room and delay sleep than to hear our special song.

"Okay, but then you must go to sleep. It's already past your bedtime."

I sing the song several times, then finally tuck her in. As I close the door behind me, I am reminded of the end of that first day together in China.

My first day of motherhood had been difficult and exhausting. Jade was resistant at first, but eventually decided she could trust me. She clung desperately to me, as if I were her lifeline, screaming if I let her out of my arms for even a moment. That night, I placed her in the crib next to my neighboring bed, much to her protestations. I quickly lay on my bed facing her, with just the mesh side of the Chinese crib dividing us. I placed my hand on the black plastic, inviting her palm to join my own. We traced hearts and clouds until she drifted off to sleep.

"*Wo ai ni*," I whispered to my delicate new daughter, hoping that a corner of her consciousness was still awake enough to receive my message.

Every night of the next week and a half spent in China, I whispered my love to sleeping Jade. She would lie there, unchanged, her chest continuing to rise and fall with each breath. I continued to look for a sign that she knew I was her mother, that I was her protector, guide, and friend forever. But I was disappointed to find that she appeared exactly the same after I said those words as she did before.

"*Wo ai ni*, precious Jade," I whispered into the air.

The last day of our China journey finally came. All of the families at the White Swan Hotel boarded buses headed to the U.S. Consulate's office in Guangzhou. Everyone was excited about the official swearing-in ceremony that would enable our Chinese children to become U.S. citizens upon their arrival in the States. The room was packed with expectant families, all waiting to swear that the paperwork we had submitted was truthful.

As the ceremony began, I looked down in my lap to find a sleeping Jade.

"Should we wake her?" I asked Kevin.

"No, let her sleep. She'll understand all of this one day."

When it was over, we were given Jade's visa and told that we were now free to go home. Kevin and I hugged, and then kissed our peacefully napping daughter. We hurried outside to meet the driver who was transporting us to the airport for our flight back to Los Angeles. I held Jade close to my chest as we made our way through crowds of Americans thrilled to be headed home. We climbed into the van and drove to the airport, Jade still asleep on my lap.

"*Wo ai ni*, new daughter," I whispered.

As we neared our final destination in China, tears began to pour down my face as I fully grasped the magnitude of our good fortune.

Our young Chinese guide looked me in the eye and said, "This child is so lucky to be yours. She will be an only child in an American family. She will lack for nothing."

"Especially love," I added. "We are the lucky ones. We had to go halfway around the world, but we managed to find the perfect child for our family. She's everything we had ever dreamed our daughter would be."

As our plane began its journey homeward, I realized that sometimes it takes the innocence of a child to remind us of our universality. We each begin exactly like Jade, chest rising and falling as we sleep, oblivious to the love sent through the air by our mothers, both those who give us birth and those born in other lands. On this day of vows, I vowed to continue filling the air with love, keeping vigil, until Jade, along with the remainder of the yearning world, awakened just in time to hear the latest whisper. One day, perhaps Jade will launch her own whisper of love to the wind, destined to reach her own sleeping child.

"*Wo ai ni*, sweet Jade," I whisper one last time through her closed door.

"Wannie, too!" she shouts back with glee bright enough to wake our entire catatonic world.

—*Cathy Crenshaw Doheny*

The Company
of Angels

In a small city on top of a mountain that was plagued by drought and overrun by conservatism, there lived a small woman who was weary and sometimes sad. She woke in pain every day, bent over by aching joints and a head that never ceased to thrum hotly in the background of her life. Yet, this life of hers was fine, she thought. She had work, menial but honest and not too difficult for her weakened body to perform. Her garden ran over with rampant shrubs and climbing roses, and evergreen ivy slithered and wound its way down the outside walls of her tidy little house. Friends came and went through her front door, leaving with smiles and warmth. Yes, life was not too bad.

Sometimes, though, she longed for someone to pamper her, to look after her when she was in pain and to protect her from time to time, from the harshness of the world outside. A lifetime of nurturing others, though rewarding and full, could be lonely and thankless, and the small woman wished, though not often, for someone to take the load off her, to make the tea or run her a bath. This wistfulness passed quickly, as she brushed off thoughts the way she brushed cobwebs from the corners of the kitchen. After all, people notice cobwebs long before they notice heartache.

But somewhere, hidden from sight, an angel was watching. She was a pretty cherub with round, dark eyes and Botticelli skin. A thick swatch of black hair fell beguilingly over one side of her face, and the angel, because she was so shy and unassuming, liked to hide behind her fringe.

One Friday, the small woman came home from a doctor's appointment with deep shadows cutting across the planes of her pale face. She was bone-weary and ill. Seeing the small woman from the hallway, where the concerned cherub often quietly watched and waited, the angel could take no more. Stepping into the foyer, she took the small woman by the hand and led her to the living room, telling her simply to "sit." Somewhat perplexed but too tired to protest, the small woman sat. Then, leaving her with instructions to do nothing, not even to move a muscle, except perhaps to breathe, the angel left the room.

Soon, the sound of running water and the faint fragrance of lavender wafted down the hallway, dancing delectably on the small woman's nostrils. She squirmed. She wanted to see what the angel was doing, but the angel appeared in the doorway, gave her a firm look, and told her to be patient.

A few moments later, the angel took the small woman's hand once again and led her to the ramshackle bathroom, which had, to the woman's surprise, been transformed into a magical place of candlelight and strange mists. The angel told the small woman to sink into the bath and to stay there for at least half an hour.

"But where is my towel, dear?"

The angel simply shook her head.

"And my pajamas? Could I—?"

"No," stated the angel with calm authority. "Just sit."

Again, the baffled woman sat, easing into the warm water with a grateful sigh.

The angel reappeared, bringing with her sweet meditation music, which played on and on until the small woman was woozy with delight and lost in a world where tea-light candles were fireflies, dripping walls were waterfalls, and mystical castles floated by on clouds of steam. From somewhere in the distance came the rustle of wings, a flutter of feathers, and the faint sound of singing.

After a time, the angel brought in the woman's towel and pajamas, both soft and warmed, and held them out lovingly for the small woman to take. She didn't mind seeing the small woman naked, for angels don't mind those earthly things.

When she was dried and dressed, the woman emerged, floating into the kitchen on clouds of exotic oils, her body soothed and the pain in her shoulders miraculously gone. Before her, a feast was in preparation. The angel stood and faced her, jealously guarding the scene.

"Uh-uh, don't touch anything!" she directed.

The woman hovered over her, anxious to help and wanting to put things away or wipe up spills. But, still under the angel's spell, she did as she was told. She watched as a chilled bottle of wine appeared. The angel, blushing, said she had never opened a bottle of wine before and did the small woman mind doing just that one little thing?

"Not at all," said the woman. Feeling useful at last, she popped the cork and reached for a glass on the shelf.

"Wait a minute!" the angel cut in. "There's a chilled wine flute in the freezer."

And so the evening proceeded. The meal was a three-course delight with dimmed lights and pleasant company—for there is no better company than an angel.

Once the woman was replete and dozy, the angel again took her by the hand and tucked her in bed. The pillows were plumped and a thick quilt was pulled up under her chin, then the soft-eyed cherub slid into bed beside her, wrapping the small, weary woman in her arms. And there they lay, the happiest of beings, snuggled together like mother and daughter . . . which, in case you haven't already guessed it, is exactly what they were. For the angel is my seventeen-year-old daughter and I the small, weary woman. My angel did all this for me one Friday night, even though she was sick with a heavy cold herself, had been to school all day, and had attended a community meeting until 6:00 P.M. She often performs these random acts of kindness, not just for me but for her whole family, friends, and even strangers. She is a shining light, and I am richly blessed to have her as my daughter, my angel.

—Melinda Jensen

Uh-Oh, Here Comes
the Cheerio Mom!

I had a classmate in fourth grade named Susie whose mother used to pack her the perfect lunch. There were no crusts on her Wonder Bread; her sandwich was neatly trimmed into four perfect corners. She had a Ding Dong or a Twinkie everyday, potato chips, fresh fruit, and a tikki punch that her mother had removed from the freezer at just the right time so that by lunch it was a refreshing icy frappe she could sip in the sun.

Meanwhile, my lunches were what you might call a grab bag. I was never quite sure what would be in there. My parents both worked outside the home, so they had to throw lunches together for three kids in the morning, and sometimes it was pretty obvious they were not only stretching groceries but also in a hurry. You knew times were tough when your sandwich included two heals of bread and your fruit selection was a beefsteak tomato.

Sometimes I would ask my mom if we could just buy the things Susie had in her lunch. She would occasionally oblige, but Twinkies wouldn't last a day in our house, especially once Dad got home. We'd wait anxiously for Mom to go to bed, then he would sneak them out of the cupboard and we would devour them in front of the television. It was all so naughty and fun—like giggling through a church service. I am sure Mom heard it all from the other room.

Susie was also a Girl Scout. When she wore her uniform to school, it was neatly pressed with a sash across her chest and adorned with patches representing her numerous accomplishments. Her knee socks were always new, and even her ponytail holder was the right shade of green to match her uniform. Her outfits on remaining days were just that—outfits. She had a number of cardigans to match her wide assortment of plaid skirts and starched blouses. Her hair was perfectly parted, and her patent leather shoes were always sparkly and clean.

When our washer and dryer were out of operation (which was often), my mom would take our clothes to a launderette after work. One evening, she left the basket on top of her car, and we had to walk through the neighborhood to find what to wear in the morning. As far as I could tell, Susie's mom paid a lot of attention to detail, while mine had somehow decided details were not important. I never resented my mother for this, but I certainly made comparisons and wondered what it would be like to have a Wonder Bread sandwich and matching socks every day.

In fifth grade, there was some sort of PTA scandal going on. I wasn't sure what the big controversy was, but I knew a large contingent of parents was protesting and making waves in the community. I remember my folks calling them "book burners." At the helm of the operation was Susie's mother—who, on the surface, appeared as polished as her daughter but, upon closer examination, looked wide-eyed and ready to snap. She came to open house with flyers in hand, ready to solicit new members for her crusade against all things deemed inappropriate. My parents smiled at her and quickly moved on.

In the car I heard Mom whisper to Dad that she feared Susie's mother was becoming a "Cheerio Mom."

"What's a 'Cheerio Mom?'" I inquired.

"I'll explain another time," my mom replied, but the reference stuck with me.

Apparently, when my sisters and I were just babies, my dad worked during the day and went to school at night, leaving Mom home with no car and three kids. She and several other mothers in the neighborhood were in the same situation, so they relied on each other a great deal. It wasn't easy raising kids all on their own, but they got through it together. However, there was one mom in the group, Muriel, who always seemed to have everything under control. Her children were neat and perfect; her house was neat and perfect; even the dog was a pure-bred masterpiece. Much like Susie's mom, Muriel was the Martha Stewart of the neighborhood, and nothing ever seemed to rattle her. My mom marveled at her poise and perfection as she handled every aspect of motherhood and homemaking with style and finesse.

One afternoon, Mom came home and stopped in her tracks at the sight of a large white wagon in Muriel's driveway. Her husband had come home for lunch and found Muriel sitting in the middle of the kitchen floor, throwing handfuls of Cheerios over her head and yelling "Wee! Wee! Weeeeee!" Muriel had officially lost her mind—snapped, cracked, and unraveled in the monotony and pressure of it all— and was admitted to a mental hospital. Although we moved to a new neighborhood shortly thereafter, my mom never forgot the story about the "Cheerio Mom," often remembering her with both fondness and concern.

Soon, the women's movement was in full force, and my mother embraced her role as an independent thinker. She never closed herself off to the changing times and always chose freedom over order. She got her master's degree, went back to work, and preached to her three daughters the importance of self-confidence and equal rights. Our household pretty much reflected her "anything goes" approach to life, and while I might have wanted Susie's sandwich every now and then, I was proud of my mom. She was a free spirit and encouraged that quality in everyone.

Through the years, the term "Cheerio Mom" became a catch-all phrase to describe all those times when we take life too seriously and lose ourselves in the process.

Ironically, I have become a stay-at-home mom. Even though I was raised to think unconventionally, my husband and I have a system that is working right now, and I have chosen to stay home with the kids. I love it. However, I don't know how I would be able to do this happily without the influence of my fiercely independent mother. Her first words of advice when my son was born were prefaced with heartfelt love and congratulations but nonetheless included a sincere admonition: "Remember the Cheerio Mom." In other words, keep being you. Even if it means sloppy lunches and wrinkled clothes, stand firm and know what matters.

It's amazing to me how hard it is not to be a Cheerio Mom. It really is tempting to have everything in order all of the time. It creates such a sense of control, albeit false. But what my mom learned early on from poor Muriel and passed on to me is that there is a Cheerio Mom in us all needing to break free before she completely breaks down. Although we are, indeed, in charge and keeping watch as mothers, we cannot control the tides, temper the waves, or predict impending storms. We can only do our best to be at our best each day, hopefully ready and refreshed from a good night's rest. And getting that rest usually means leaving something undone—the laundry, the lunches, or the pile of mail waiting to be sorted.

My mom and I talk every day. This blessing does not go unappreciated. We lost my father many years ago and understand how fragile life can be. It's important to seize those moments and opportunities to really tell someone how special they are.

Thank you, Mom, for lunches full of leftovers and shoe laces fashioned from twine, for letting us build forts in the house and play in your closet, for making pancakes for dinner and letting me drink coffee (which was really just cream and sugar), for taking us to the beach all summer and watching us run wild through the surf, for buying a yogurt maker and teaching me macaroni art, and so much more. Thank you, Mom, for living and giving me a life outside the Cheerio box.

—Shawn Lutz

Quick Bright Thing

My son Gideon, sixth-grade graduate, pops open the wallpaper paste and plucks the seal from the applicator. We are in the smallest room of the house that my husband and I and our two young sons moved to nearly twenty years ago.

While I'm decoding the instructions, Gideon squeezes the bottle of paste. A blob splashes to the floor.

"Slow down," I say, grabbing paper towels.

I look up at the wall and notice the glue stains still visible where, years after we moved in, I pasted up a wallpaper border of rainbows in bright primary colors to convert the guest room into a child's bedroom. I can still picture my awkward, pregnant self, too impatient to wait for my husband to help me, tottering on the stepstool, struggling with glue and sponge, to hang these rainbows in delicious anticipation of my third son, Gideon.

The rainbows were my choice, but today's job is all Gideon's doing.

"I'm too old for rainbows!" he said last fall when sixth-grade graduation seemed years away.

All winter and spring I resisted, pretending that this child of my forties would occupy his childhood bedroom forever, as his two brothers, now both away at college, had not. But one June day, his lips stained with the juice of the strawberries we'd picked together that morning, Gideon brought it up again. This time, I couldn't put him off.

At the home decor shop, among the fat wallpaper books, I pointed out the astronauts, soccer balls, nautical maps. But, shaking his head, Gideon opened his strawberry-tinted mouth and said, "Nah. I'll know it when I see it." Then, his eyes widening, "This one."

And here it is, scrolling out onto the wall, a pattern I never expected: a row of palm trees. Nothing like the crayon colors of the old rainbows, the palm trees' colors are muted, olive, ochre, honey, and wheat, trunks freestanding, fronds reaching up and out.

I ask Gideon why he chose this pattern. His only answer is a shrug.

We climb ladders side by side. From here, I notice the new elongation in his arms and legs, the new sharpness in his cheekbones.

I used to think of this youngest son as the icing on the cake. The icing's role is to be sweet and cute. And he was.

When Gideon was a baby, my husband, two older sons, and I sang him "Twinkle, Twinkle, Little Star," knowing exactly which lyrics ("Up above the world so high") ignited his one-tooth grin, which in turn lit up ours. He invented his own name for me; to this child, I was "Mimi." When he was three and a half, he and I spent a summer afternoon pitching stones into the creek. Squealing at each splash, Gideon lisped into my ear, "I love you more than throwing rocks in the water." I didn't care if he read at age four, five, or six or if he knew his times tables or scored a goal in soccer; I enjoyed him, uncomplicated by expectations.

But now, the icing aspires for more.

In fifth grade, he e-mailed his teacher three whole weeks before a civics test: "Please clarify the pocket veto."

I have no head for numbers, so I marveled when Gideon brought home perfect scores on math tests, beaming, "The teacher says I might be an engineer!"

When he was in sixth grade, I watched him memorize over 300 cities, rivers, and mountains on his world map, spreading his papers across the kitchen table, earnestly prodding, "Quiz me again!"

Last spring, Gideon, in tunic and leggings as Lysander in the sixth-grade production of *A Midsummer Night's Dream*, touched the shoulder of his twelve-year-old Hermia and delivered his abridged-version lines: *"Since, if there were a sympathy in choice / War, death or sickness did lay siege to it / Making it momentary as a sound / So quick bright things come to confusion."*

He is becoming a leaner, more chiseled version of himself. I see it not just in his body but in his actions, in this new determination and independence. And, like the wallpaper, it's all Gideon's doing.

Gideon on one ladder, I on the other, we climb over each other in a complicated dance that reflects our mother-son relationship. He steadies the roll while I slather the paste. I approximate the paper onto the paste; he smoothes it with the sponge, passes the sponge to me, descends, slides his ladder over, and scrambles up again on my other side to take the dangling end from my hand. And so we leapfrog over each other.

I think to myself, *He runs ahead to jump right over me as I drag my ladder behind.*

The palm trees overtake the rainbows. Fronds reach like hands, fingers spread wide, pinkies and thumbs nearly but not quite touching each other. I wonder, *Is that why they're called palm trees, because they resemble open hands?*

Two feet from the corner where we started, we run out of wallpaper. We look at each other.

"I never was much good at measuring," I admit.

We'll have to order an entire new roll to cover those last two feet and finish another day.

We stand back to look. Even incomplete, the palm trees bring out the honey window shades and the July sunlight spilling onto the bed. Two feet of rainbows remain, peeking out.

I leave the room briefly. When I return, Gideon is perched on his ladder, reaching up with scissors to snip a square of rainbow. I open my mouth, but before I can ask what he's doing, he explains, "Just in case I forget what it looked like."

Gideon, my quick bright thing. He's still surprising his mother. Even this third time around, I couldn't have predicted that at this young age he'd be so self-aware or that he, too, feels a loss as he leaves one phase of life for another. I've been underestimating my youngest son's newfound depth, just as I underestimated this room. I catch my breath, thinking, *I, too, want to cut out a snippet of rainbow to remember this moment by.*

A week later, at the day-camp circus, I'm in the audience as the director introduces the few children who have mastered the art of plate spinning. To my astonishment, Gideon is among them. Under the parachute of the big top stands Gideon, brow furrowed, jaw set, eyes intent on his task. He lifts his hand aloft, spinning a plate on the tip of his index finger. For a moment, in his vertical arm and unfurled fingers, I can feel the strength of the palm trees on his bedroom wall. He defies his mother's calculations all over again.

—Faith Paulsen

One Fat Frog and the Tyranny of Toys

It is 11:00 P.M. and Little Leapfrog is splayed on my living room floor like an unwanted guest who drank his weight in mojitos at the New Year's party. At least Froggy's lifeless green body is quiet. It's usually babbling the ABCs or spewing forth some consonant or vowel as my daughter frantically urges me to punch the letters on his stomach.

This frog helps Kate learn the alphabet. But in the process he and his blabbing brethren of talking toys are driving me insane. It's no wonder I suck down a five o'clock chardonnay to take the edge off as Lil Leap and his evil ilk count, bleat, beep, and croon.

To come clean, this is my fault. I thought these toys were educational and fun, so I registered for them. That's how the fat frog, a barn with magnetic animals, a musical Leap Table, a stuffed singing caterpillar, and a plastic pull toy caterpillar ended up in our house. I figured they'd be good enough for our thirteen-month-old.

Good enough? There's no such thing when you're an organic-obsessed, affluent San Francisco mommy with access to a Google search engine. I came to realize this mighty quickly after I ran into mommies who really do believe that plastic toys are the environment-ruining devil and talking toys his brain-development-stunting spawn.

These mommies subscribe to *Real Simple*, boycott Pampers, and line their living rooms with Haba wooden cars, natural fiber books, and Peruvian free-trade cloth dolls. They make my choice in toys just another niggling thing to worry about in the shower, along with fears that Kate's space heater would catch fire at 4:00 A.M. or that her limbs will retract because she spits up most vegetables. My fretting started after a visit to the house of a friend—a sassy, smart vegetarian who sneaks flaxseed into most everything her daughter eats to increase her brain development. She wants to start a preschool co-op so she has control over her daughter's early education. I am truly in awe of her ambition and energy. I scanned her living room floor. There was a basket of soft cloth books mixed with some wooden toys, some puppets, and an abacus. I didn't see any plastic. There was no

Little Leap Frog. No toys that talk or bleep. I did not bring this up, but when this friend e-mailed links to websites that offer all sorts of European toys that I do not own, I started to wonder about our Fisher Price and Leap Fleet. Was I missing something?

Another morning, I send Kate off to a daycare exchange with her talking "See 'n Say" wheel. The sweet boy she was visiting had played with the See 'n Say at our house the week before and loved it. When I returned to get Kate, his mom handed me the toy in a rumpled plastic bag like it was a poopy diaper. "I'm trying to get these sorts of toys out of the house," she said. She asked me not to bring such a toy again.

I was mortified but also a bit pissed off. It's just a stupid See 'n Say that makes barnyard sounds, but I refrained from telling her that out of I'm-a-chicken niceness. You'd think I'd fed her kid Safeway conventional grapes. I grabbed the bag and started to wonder why I was never briefed about the "plastic is the devil" people.

At Kate's playgroup, I asked the director, a child development professor, if these talking toys we've acquired do anything to help Kate learn.

"Kids don't necessarily need talking toys if you already talk to them a lot," she told me. Talking toys won't harm her, she added, but they are best used when a child is attention-deprived.

Attention-deprived child? Kate is definitely not attention-deprived. I talk to her all of the time. I can't shut up. If Leap Frog is doing her no harm, why should she give him up? I had a talking Mrs. Beasley when I was a kid and I turned out okay. Besides, not all her toys talk. Her favorite toy, a stuffed bear, doesn't make a peep. Her second favorite, jumbo plastic Lego blocks, are pretty quiet, too.

Little Leap is not, which is one reason why I loathe him. He is a doofy-looking thing about half her size but wider, who sings the ABCs to an exciting back beat. Kate feared him at first, whimpering when I plopped him near her. But she warmed up soon enough, inching herself closer and closer, finally directing me to push the circle on his fat finger and sing along with her—over and over and over.

I am pondering just how asinine I'd look to one of my single friends when Kate belts out an "*mmmmmmmm*" for "M" and I am momentarily happy. She is learning! She will go to Stanford early admission! She will take care of her writer parents in their toothless golden years!

Kate also adores her Farmer Tad barn, which sits on our refrigerator.

"Hi! I'm farmer Tad. Listen to my banjo!" Tad squeaks.

Never mind that there is probably no farmer in the Western Hemisphere with a stupid name like Tad, whose job it is to shepherd children as they match a horse head to the horse ass in the plastic barn.

"You made a match," Tad's associate sings when Kate does it right. "Look what you found! You made a match, hear a cow sound!"

"*Mooooo*," groans a cow that sounds drugged.

Thankfully, this toy does not sing the ABCs. It simply reinforces the strange fantasy children have of modern farming.

This is okay. And it's okay that these toys make my teeth grind, too. Kids are supposed to play with annoying toys. They're kids. I figure that, until she's in preschool, Kate and I will have a deal: she gets to keep most of her talking army (okay, I tossed out a talking Pooh Bear who begged me to pick him up one too many times and a Rock with Elmo guitar when the batteries kicked) in exchange for a ban on all toddler DVDs. That's a fair exchange, I think, even though Kate seems to hate TV. Her first brush with an Elmo video left her with a serious case of ennui. She lasted five minutes.

The next month, I attend a Super Bowl party at another friend's house. Their daughter is just a few months older than Kate, a cherubic toddler who, at two, is already speaking in sentences. Her father is a professor who specializes in child development, so I am anxious to see what sort of toys his daughter uses.

I am in luck. After the game, all the parents head into the little girl's room to sit with all the kids. I quickly scan the room. There are books. There are too many puzzles to count. Puzzles with numbers, letters, animals, shapes, butterflies. The professor confirms that puzzles are great for their brains at this age, and I don't have a problem with that.

The only problem is that, at best, Kate only has two puzzles, which means she might be falling behind, which is the fear of all urban moms everywhere. I am sure there will be a mandatory puzzle test to get her into the best preschool.

The next day, I rush to Target and find two natural-wood puzzles. One has the numbers one to twenty marked on pieces with pictures of ladybugs, balloons, flowers, and the like; the other is the letters of the alphabet.

When I get the puzzles home, I unwrap them and leave them for Kate. After ambling over to check them out, Kate immediately dumps the parts on the floor and heads to the kitchen cabinet. There, she pulls out a green plastic colander and puts it on her head. On this day, at least, she seems to prefer plastic.

—Kim Girard

This story was first published on mamazine.com.

Dance Lessons

Last weekend I helped my daughter and her roommates pack up their Manhattan apartment. I took the train down from Albany early Saturday morning, enjoying the scenic spring ride along the Hudson.

Three hours later, I walked across six avenues and eights blocks to their building. For once, I was traveling lightly, with only a backpack, because Elissa had told me I'd be bringing her skis and ski bag back upstate with me, to be tucked away until next winter. Her new place would have bigger bedrooms but smaller closets.

By the time I arrived at their fifth-floor walkup, the landing outside their door resembled a Goodwill drop-off. I stepped over three shopping bags of clothes, silk pillows, and a puffy white down coat whose arms lay open on the stairs, as if waiting for company.

The girls had been sorority sisters (Kappa Kappa Gamma) and roommates at the University of Michigan. Working women now, they'd decided, a year after graduating from college, that they were ready to upgrade their living space.

"Need any help?" I had asked a week before the scheduled move to Soho.

"Got it under control," Elissa said.

I didn't doubt it. An honors student in high school, she had gone to the university to pursue organizational studies, an interdisciplinary program combining psychology, sociology, and economics. She is practical, focused, decisive in a way I never was at her age. At twenty-two, she juggles a consulting job, apartment, boyfriend, and large circle of friends like an artistic director, making choices about what fits and what doesn't. She lives in New York on weekends and works, for the time being, in St. Louis during the week. We chat via phone, mostly when I am driving to work and she is waiting at an airport.

So I was surprised and pleased when she changed her mind about my offer of help.

"I was thinking . . ." she texted me, "it might be good to have an extra pair of hands."

All week I looked forward to the task. This would give me a chance to be an active part of my daughter's life. So often these days, I feel like a visitor.

When Elissa left for college, I suffered separation blues but knew she still needed me in concrete ways (advice, money, a home base). With school breaks, parent weekends, and other periodic visits, there hardly was time to miss her. If childrearing is the main course served to parents, then college is the palate cleanser, or *intermezzo*, giving us time to refresh ourselves, to rediscover our own passions and pleasures before our children move on.

Still, I didn't expect my daughter's transition to adult life to be such an awakening for me. I'm a mother, but my mothering isn't needed much. After two decades, how do I stop parenting? I've always loved the whirlwind of young lives, the chaos and bright commotion. I feel superfluous now. I realize this is a good thing; it means I've done the job I was supposed to do. Especially in these times, when adolescence stretches far into the twenties (or beyond), it's no small feat to launch a kid or two.

Last Saturday in New York, my hands were busy wrapping wine glasses in little Styrofoam sheaths in the kitchen. When I was finished, I joined Elissa in her bedroom.

"Need these?" she said, pointing to a row of beautiful wooden hangers in her closet. "I won't have room in my new apartment."

I took a hanger and looked around. Unopened bottles of shampoo and bath gels topped her wastebasket.

"You're getting rid of these?" I asked.

She nodded.

"The wicker end table?"

"No room."

"This nice shelving unit?"

"The new place is configured differently."

Foolish me; I thought she was moving to a larger apartment, thought that was the point. But I, who lately have taken to buying less and recycling everything I can in this age of the *frugalista*, tried not to comment or cast judgment on her choices.

The fact is, my daughter amazes me.

As I watched her climb across her soon-to-be-dismantled bed to disconnect power-surge cords, I couldn't help but flash back to another room, a different drama, seventeen years earlier . . .

I was the dance-loving mother eager to watch my daughter strut her stuff in a ballet recital. But as rows of little girls in neat hair buns leaped across the studio, Elissa was slumped in the hallway, her curly dark hair uncombed around her shoulders, leotard and gingham skirt as rumpled as her temperament. My teary five-year-old wanted none of it, and all my coaxing and shameless begging would not move her.

"Just follow!" I finally shouted.

Eventually she did, but it was a hollow victory. My usually exuberant little girl was a joyless lump on the dance floor.

As I watched her sashay through her compact apartment that weekend we packed her up in New York, I saw that Elissa choreographs her own life now with grace. She's taken her lumps—the job rejections, the summer boyfriend who turned into a toad, the responsibilities to divorced parents and dual house-holds—and keeps moving. The steps are all her own.

"I'll be back. Going to drop these at the vintage store," she said before evaporating down the clogged stairwell, arms full of clothes.

"We need more packing tape," she told me later, dispatching me to the FedEx store around the corner for yet another roll.

Though tempted to do so, I didn't point out the savings she could have accrued by buying larger rolls in the first place. This was her city, her way, her life. My job was to go with it.

"First, we deliver them into the world, then we deliver them to the world," a friend with four grown children is fond of saying.

Saturday evening, I took the girls to dinner at a pub on Third Avenue. While heading out, we ran into one of the young women who lived across the hall. Unexpectedly, she offered to give them a couch. Great—but Elissa and her roommates had already negotiated to buy a used couch (plus end tables, coffee table, and microwave) on Craigslist for $400. Nonetheless, we investigated. The proposed couch was a nondescript blue and slightly worn but otherwise acceptable.

At dinner, an ethical discussion ensued. What was the commitment to the Craigslist seller? No money had yet changed hands, but there was a verbal agreement and this stranger was moving shortly, so she had to get rid of it immediately.

My daughter struggled with this. She hated to renege, but one of her roommates saw it differently.

"Hey, if I could get a free couch, why not?" she said.

I decided not to introduce the concept of bad karma before a big move, so I sipped my beer and listened to them puzzle it out, silently thankful to note that I have raised a child with a sense of ethics.

To take the couch or not? While we ate our salads and burgers, there were text messages, phone calls, questions about how to proceed, last-minute negotiations that made Wall Street trading seem like child's play. They needed to reach the one girl who was the actual owner for final approval.

The owner called. The freebee, it turned out, came at a price. There would be a chopping charge. In New York, there is a whole niche market devoted to chopping sofas; that is, sawing them in parts and later reassembling them to fit through doorways and other tight spaces. The girls across the hall paid a sofa doctor $200 when they moved in. Now, they were eager to unload the couch because soon they, too, would be moving and they weren't eager to pay for more furniture surgery.

Thanks, but no thanks, my daughter said.

The next morning, while her roommates went off to brunch, Elissa and I tackled the hall closet.

"Are you taking this dryer rack?" I said, somewhat hopefully. It looked unused.

She shook her head. Ditto the extra silverware, the package of light bulbs, the Swiffer.

We removed her air conditioning unit from its window casement without it falling and pummeling passersby five floors below. Pulling it out together made me unreasonably happy. She really did need an extra pair of hands—my hands.

Next, I watched as she deconstructed her stubborn, queen-size bed frame using equal parts hammer and fingernails. She was in charge of this one. And when her roommates returned, Elissa unflinchingly trashed carcasses of dead rodents from behind their couch (which they had agreed to sell to someone else on Craigslist) with only one short but well-pitched squeal as the others looked on.

Hours after we'd packed up everything, I headed back upstate, relieved at how much we'd accomplished in a day and a half. But the drama was not over yet.

"Disaster!" Elissa texted me when I was minutes from home.

The girls were all packed up and ready to go. They'd carried many boxes down five flights to expedite things. But the New Jersey moving man was missing in action.

"He's way late," Elissa texted me again.

By the time the girls relinquished all hope of him appearing, it was nine o'clock Sunday evening and Elissa was due on a plane to St. Louis at eight the next morning. Everything she owns was sitting in boxes in her apartment or in the courtyard downstairs.

The clock was ticking. She called a dozen U-Haul companies in the Big Apple (why had she ever agreed to a firm from Jersey?), but it was the last weekend of the month—prime moving time in a city of millions.

More than 100 miles away, while I Googled "Man with a Van, NYC" and anxiously awaited word, Elissa spun into action. A few false starts and several hours later, she had contacted a new moving service, checked in with her boss, updated her flight arrangements.

The move went on.

That reluctant, sullen ballerina from a childhood ago had transformed into a decisive young woman executing not the flawless arabesque but a pretty impressive furniture fandango.

When I think about that weekend now, I realize it's taken me a while to accept that my daughter wasn't born to fill my needs or replicate my desires, but to shape her own. Not an easy lesson, but a necessary one. As I listen and marvel, once again at the sidelines, I realize I have managed to raise a daughter who can dance, after all.

—*Tina Lincer*

Tiaras and Rhinestones

The day I first realized how lucky I was to have a mom like mine, I was wearing a patch on my left eye. Blue eyeglasses sat upon my freckled face. But not just any old blue eyeglasses. I wore blue eyeglasses—with rhinestones.

I had a lazy eye when I was a child and needed to wear an eye-patch over my right "good" eye in order to work out the muscles in my left "bad" eye, which tended to roam. When I was told about the patch in the optometrist's office, I looked up at the ceiling (or the ceiling and the wall, in my case) and let out a great big sigh. Wasn't having to wear glasses bad enough for a six-year-old? How would I face the kids at school with new glasses—and a patch on my eye?

My mind quickly turned to the little girl in my class who had told me, after I'd recently had a bad haircut, that she wouldn't be talking to me for awhile, because her mom had taught her that "if she had nothing nice to say, to say nothing at all."

So, while the eye doctor showed my mom how to stick the patch on my eye, I pouted. She would have to change the patch (which looked like a big, round Band-Aid) daily until the muscles got strong.

With my new patch in place, I made my way to the other room—with half the world now blacked out around me—and set out to choose my new glasses. My mom stood next to me as I sat on a tall black stool with my legs dangling. I squinted and looked back and forth and up and down along the display wall until I finally saw them. At first I thought I was seeing some kind of mirage as the light reflected against the pretty, glittering blue frames. But it was no mirage. There they were, second row from the top: powder-blue glasses with little rhinestones. Speechless, I leaned over the counter and pointed to the gemmed beauties hanging there among the other simple, less fancy, average, not so powder-blue-with-little rhinestone glasses.

The optometrist placed them on my nose and over my patched eye. I looked into the oval mirror on the counter and was surprised to find a girl I didn't know. I smiled at her and she smiled back. I turned to my mom, who gave me a nod of approval and a thumbs-up to the optometrist. The choice had

been made, and there now sat a little girl with freckles, an eye patch, and glasses made for a princess. No
nasty comment from any little brat at school could
deny that I looked beautiful.

Soon after that day, I was sitting at my desk in
school wearing my new princess glasses, my mom's
clip-on earrings, and a sequined tiara that I had gotten for Christmas. I had dressed myself that day. We
were usually in a rush in the morning, as my mom
worked two jobs since my dad had left the family.
We got dressed, ate a quick bowl of cereal, and my
brother and I headed off to school.

Sometimes we had no car, and sometimes my
mom drove my uncle's old Dodge Challenger,
which roared like a tank. On those random days
when Mom would get the engine to turn over, we
would drive to school. I would sit on the floor of
the car as she drove, too embarrassed to be seen in
the car with its offensive noise that came from the
muffler—or lack thereof.

But all was fine on that particular day as I sat in
class with my baby-blue rhinestone eyeglasses, my
mom's earrings, and my tiara. Not rain nor snow
nor a noisy tank nor a classroom brat would darken
my day. Yes, all was well with the world as far as I
was concerned, even though my teacher had a confused and slightly annoyed look on her face. She had

looked at me that way a few times that day. I was thinking maybe she wished she had a tiara to wear, too, and wondering whether I might have to lend it to her, when suddenly she blurted out:

"Does your mother know what you're wearing to school?"

I had never seen such jealousy on display. I assured her that the lovely earrings were not mine and only a borrowed item from my mother.

When school let out and the parents came to pick up us kids, my mom pulled up in the tank and waved to me, standing at the school's door. As I walked toward the car, my teacher made a beeline for my mother. I thought it was a bit tacky for a teacher to ask to borrow my mother's clip-on earrings (germs and all) right there in broad daylight.

"Do you know your child wore your jewelry and a tiara to school?" the teacher asked my mother.

My freckled face turned beet red as I was overcome with a wave of shock and embarrassment. From her tone I could tell that she was not jealous but rather ticked off and that perhaps I looked silly.

I knew Mom had been in a rush that morning. Maybe she didn't really look at me very well. Maybe I showed her the earrings while she was getting dressed and her permission was more of a "Wear whatever, just get dressed" response. And now, there

I was, in front of my teacher, my classmates, and their parents, wondering what on Earth my mother was going to say to my teacher?

As I held my breath, my mom—who is always cool under the most uncomfortable of circumstances, looked at me and back to the teacher. Then in an even but pleasant voice she said, "Yes, of course I knew about the earrings; I lent them to her myself.

"I think Mary looks lovely," she added with a smile.

I let out my breath, relieved. But I need not have worried. My mom was always there for me—even when I stepped out of line. She always made me feel beautiful—even when it may not have been the case. Though I realize now that my mother struggled to keep our family afloat, as a child I never felt poor or that I lacked anything. And I always knew that, in my mother's eyes, I was a princess.

So how does a girl who grows up with no money and an absent father and who drives around on the floor of a tank learn to love herself and succeed in life? With blue rhinestone glasses and a mom like mine.

—*Mary C. M. Phillips*

Why Today
Is Jammie Day

My three-year-old son is in his jammies. This is not really a bad thing. In fact, it is a rather endearing sight. Clad comfortably in pants and a shirt with a pattern of various earth-moving vehicles scattered on a field of blue, accessorized by the red socks he pulled from his dresser last night—the kind of socks that are long enough to be rolled down for a "triple-cuff" but are now unfurled happily midway up his tiny calves—he bears a striking resemblance to a superhero.

The problem with this vision in blue is the timing or, more precisely, the time—10:43 A.M. on a Friday. It is a bit late, outside of a college campus or an episode of *Desperate Housewives*, to still be in jammies. And, as the parent charged with my son's well-being between the hours of, say, 8 A.M. and 6 P.M., this lack of social grace is entirely my responsibility. But before you judge me (and rightly so), hear me out.

Before I can send my superhero to his phone booth with instructions to emerge in an outfit more suited to midday life in suburbia, he really, really should have a bath. No, really. Good manners, good hygiene, and the local health department all dictate this, and the health department doesn't even know about my husband's experiment last night at dinner to see if our son really is an ambidextrous eater (he is not) or my son's own experiment with the "shield" on his potty (don't ask). The reasons my son needs a bath are clear; the logic is simple. The process is anything but. In order to give my son a bath, I must, in all good conscience, first clean the bathtub.

Now, I am hardly obsessive about germs, but even I know when enough is enough. And when plastic purple porpoises and rubber ducks jump back out of the bathwater, it's time to scrub. But after I scrub, I will need a large plastic cup that I can use for the rinsing process, since our tub is not equipped with one of those magnificent spigot-sprayer-attachment-type things, and my husband and I have a fear of plumbing that precludes us from installing one. The problem is that the large cup already sitting on the side of the bathtub has been sitting on the side of the bathtub since the purple porpoise, and possibly my son, were both very young.

When I toss the science experiment into the trash can, however, with plans to retrieve a new one from our collection (did we register at Taco Bell when we were first married? Or when we became parents?), I notice that the trash is full. Easily remedied, except that when I pull the trash bag from the container, I notice that it has just enough room left in it to hold the dirty diapers idling down the hall in the nursery trash can. (I never mastered a Diaper Genie or any of its well-meaning cousins.)

Alas, when I reach the nursery trash can, located conveniently beside the changing table, I notice the pile of clean clothes sitting on top of the changing table. Seizing the opportunity and remembering the 2:00 A.M. changing in the middle of the nursery floor, I attempt to put away the clothes.

Unfortunately, I soon realize that the clothes were on the changing table because there was no room in the closet, which I now must reorganize. I hastily try to sort the overflowing garments into piles: too big, too small, keep, cherish, donate (note to self: find some creative way to "cherish"—make quilt in spare time?).

When I take the pile for "donate" back down the hall to the master bedroom walk-in closet, I find the shopping bag kept there for such occasions. I also find, however, that my husband has generously "donated" his own sweaty gym clothes to a different corner of the closet. I marvel at his inability to walk five steps to the laundry chute—after all, he had the stamina to work out, right?—and I hoist the pile to the open chute door.

That is when I realize what my husband already knew: the clothes in the two-story chute are jammed to eye level. I go downstairs to start a load of clothes, emptying the chute and using an inverted broom to dislodge the clothes stuck halfway up the house.

After I have unburied myself from the pile of dirty clothes, I realize that, as long as the broom is out and in my hands, I can no longer ignore the dust bunnies grabbing at my ankles as I walk through the first floor of our home. And now that I have swept, it would be irresponsible and lazy not to follow up with a thorough and judicious mopping. Or a Swiffer WetJet.

Unfortunately, the clean floor highlights the fact that my countertops appear textured even though they are not, and I have no choice but to pull out the modern mom's greatest weapon: pop-up kitchen wipes. However, good as they are, the wipes do not take care of every mark, and I am forced to go to the save-it-for-special-occasions-because-it-will-make-you-want-to-tackle-all-kinds-of-strange-marks tool: the Mr. Clean Magic Eraser.

Sure enough, as soon as I remove the mystery spot from the front of the booster seat, my eyes cannot stop finding all sorts of needs for the Magic Eraser—scuff marks on the floor, hieroglyphics on the wall, smudges on the door frame that really are too high up to belong to my son. I am in The Zone. I am zigging and zagging, wetting and wiping, removing all proof of my true standards of housekeeping.

And then I remember. The place where this cleaning tool really shines is on the glass shower door in the master bathroom. I really need to clean that bathroom. I have been meaning to get to it, especially the shower door.

But it's getting late. It's past lunchtime now, and the baby needs to eat and the dog hasn't been let out—and in and out and in—and the water jug guy is coming today and I haven't even had a shower yet. Besides, when I clean the door, the only way for me to rinse it is with a big plastic cup.

And so it is 3:42 on a Friday afternoon. And I am living with a superhero.

—*Heather K. Smith*

Thanksgiving
at Jennifer's

"Mom, I'll have Thanksgiving this year." My daughter's declaration was music to my ears. I'd hosted Thanksgiving dinner for more than thirty years. Time for a change. What a delight to have children old enough to put on a holiday feast.

"What can I bring, dear?"

"Well, how about bringing a turkey—maybe two. I think we'll have twenty to twenty-five."

Where did all the people come from? Forty years ago, it was just my husband and me.

Jennifer continued, "I'm not very good at gravy; it always lumps. Could you bring that too?"

Well, that makes sense, I thought. *I'll be the one with the turkey juice to make the gravy.*

Before I could get an "okay" out of my mouth, she added, "Maybe you could make the mashed potatoes too. You know I'm not very good at peeling potatoes.

Oh, and could you bring that dressing you always make—the one with the water chestnuts, celery, and sage?"

"Uh . . ."

"Oh, I almost forgot, could you bring your home-made rolls? It just wouldn't be Thanksgiving without those rolls. And don't forget your strawberry preserves."

Why had I even opened my mouth? I could see I would be cooking for days before Thanksgiving. So far, the only difference between this Thanksgiving and any other was that I could postpone the deep cleaning until nearer Christmas. How could I fit my job in around all these duties? Of one thing I was certain: by the time all the other guests brought a dish, no one would go home hungry.

On the Saturday before Thanksgiving, the phone rang. It was Jennifer again.

"Mom, I want to serve the food buffet-style from the dining room table. I need you to make curtains for the windows."

She had been in the house for a year and a half. It wasn't an issue before. Why should it bother her now?

"How about something simple," she went on. "Just swags. No drapes or anything. It's only about a ten-foot-wide window. I don't have any material or rods yet, but if I came over today, do you suppose we could find some fabric to match the wallpaper?"

"Uh . . . sure, honey," I said, secretly hoping we wouldn't find anything that pleased her.

First, we visited Stein-Mart. My luck held; nothing suited "our needs." At Hancock's, I ran out of luck—just as the store was closing at six. The clerk rolled off eleven yards of green fabric and another measurement of off-white lining while they turned out the lights. I stood in the checkout line. From the bolts of material behind me, I heard Jennifer's voice.

"Look, Mom! Here's a pretty window treatment on this box of rods. Will you do them like this?"

The only time I had to work on the project was on Sunday. I would do what I could.

When we came home from shopping, Jennifer popped open the trunk and pulled out two more bolts of fabric I'd not seen before. With a smile she said, "If you have time, could you work this into something for the bedroom and living room? Just a simple drape will do behind the bed. The drapes can hang from the top of that ten-foot ceiling to the floor. I don't know what to do in the living room, but I'm sure you can come up with something."

At that point, I seriously considered hugging her around the neck . . . until she turned blue.

That evening, it didn't take long to figure out that the drapes pictured on the box weren't going to work with the amount of material we'd bought. Plan B: a regular swag with jabots at the ends. I'd have to talk my husband, Vic, into making a small, L-shaped cornice board to go at the top of the ten-foot-long window. I had plan B cut out before bedtime.

After work on Monday, I started on the swags for the dining room and asked Jennifer to stop by the next day for her approval before I sewed it. Then I cut out the red bedroom drapes with care because I had to match the fruit pattern in the material. After work Tuesday, I sewed the red drapes. Jennifer came to my house to see the dining room creations. She brought two of her children—just in time for dinner.

"When will you be out tomorrow to hang them, Mom?"

"I have to work in the morning. I'll not make it to your house before two."

On Wednesday morning, I popped the turkey in the oven to bake while I went to work. I called Vic to pick up the smoked turkey at Fritz's Meat Market by six. By five, I'd set up my sewing machine in Jennifer's kitchen. Shortly, the drapes were ready to hang. Now, we needed Vic to come from work, make the small cornice board for the dining room, and hang the two sets of drapes before tomorrow. Jennifer lived forty minutes from town, so I knew we wouldn't see him any time soon.

Another small glitch. Before Vic arrived, Jennifer discovered the boards she'd bought to hang the swags on were the wrong size. We made an emergency trip to the nearest lumberyard, ten miles away, to buy different ones. Vic didn't arrive until seven. You could almost see the steam coming out his ears; he had been number sixty-two in line to pick up the smoked turkey.

After he constructed the wooden cornice, Jennifer; Vic; and Jennifer's husband, Scott, hung the ten-foot bedroom drapes. Meanwhile, I stapled the swags and jabots to the cornice board for the dining room. By ten, the hanging crew moved into the dining room for the last hurrah.

"Wife! You put these on the wrong side!"

Sure enough, I'd put the swags on what my husband intended to be the back side of the cornice board.

Scott said, "Oh, we'll just have to fix them tomorrow."

I grabbed a screwdriver to pry out each staple. Tomorrow was Thanksgiving; no time for curtain hanging then. Without another word, Jennifer took the other screwdriver and pried staples from the opposite end. By ten forty-five, we had the swags reattached and hung above the window.

I dozed in the car on the way home while Vic drove. Once home, I fell into a sound sleep the minute my head hit the pillow.

The next morning, we made the trip back to the country with the cooked turkey on my lap. Our granddaughter peeled potatoes. I made dressing, gravy, and rolls. And I remembered the preserves. Everything went off without a hitch. Next year, though, I think I'll just tell Jennifer I'll have Thanksgiving at my house.

—Sally Jadlow

Three P.M.

It is one of my favorite parts of the day: 3:00 P.M.—time to pick up DJ from kindergarten. I'm his best girl. My oldest daughter, Andrea, no longer needs me to pick her up and only occasionally acknowledges having parents. She used to get excited about me, just like DJ does now.

After class each day, standing at the doorway of the school, DJ begins the search for me. As his eyes find me, his expression turns from solemn to delighted. It's the same look he gives the train at the zoo. As soon as he finds a path through the other kids and parents, he runs over and jumps into my arms, simultaneously telling me the news of the day.

"I got to be the helper today. Michael sat next to me. I missed you." Quick kiss. "Trina threw up and it smelled really bad. I learned the stegosaurs had a brain the size of a walnut; no wonder they're dead."

On his especially spirited days, I know to get my footing, because while he is airborne he yells, "Monkey hug!" as forty-four pounds of delight slam into me. He lands at my waist and wraps his legs around.

We have other routines too. In the morning, the rule is that it has to be light outside before he is allowed to wiggle in between his parents for a morning snuggle.

His sleeping face has lost its baby fat. His long dark eyelashes almost touch the freckles that are scattered over his cheeks and nose. His nose is no longer a little round button, but a boy nose with a tip and little flares to the nostrils. A fountain of dark blond hair spews out of the crown of his head. He will want me to brush his hair when he wakes up, because "Dad can't get the sticking-up part to go down." When he speaks, his baby teeth are beginning to look small between his full red lips.

"I'm going to wear my snow pants today, so I can play wild at recess. My hair looks good, thanks."

After his breakfast of toast and fruit and a few laughs with the Rug Rats cartoon show, he's off to school for seven hours. We are reunited again at 3:00 P.M.

Today, DJ is at the back of the line. His eyes meet mine as we smile our jubilant smiles and wave. There are so many other parent-child reunions between us that there is no clear path. He runs around them all, choosing to scale a huge mountain of snow, keeping his eyes on me and a smile on his face up the eight-foot summit. As he crests the top, he breaks his gaze with me and takes inventory of his position. He is king of the mountain. He jumps up and down and gives the snow bank his joy. By the time he finishes and makes his way to me, he awards me only a casual greeting.

I'm tempted to feel disappointment, and remember Andrea and her progression away from me. By sixth grade, she always seemed angry, although "nothing" was ever wrong. She didn't want to be seen with me: "Drop me off a block from school." Her middle-school news of the day: "It was fine."

Andrea has finished high school, is weeks away from college graduation, and is about to move to her first apartment. She forgets to greet me most days and is ready to be out on her own. She loves me, and we will discover our adult relationship after she has established her own territory.

Looking down at DJ, I understand that we two are on a similar journey. My job now is to find the same joy in watching him jump in the snow as when he jumps into my arms. It is also my job to find him more snow banks to happily conquer on his path away from me and toward adulthood.

But tomorrow when I pick him up, I pray he'll jump into my arms one more time.

—*Amy Lou Jenkins*

Keeper of the Sash

Once upon a time, my charming teenage daughter reigned as a small town Apple Queen. Chosen by committee, honored by community, she lived as temporary royalty for one long year. Everyone in the kingdom recognized her by the crisp white sash she wore. At first, The Queen took splendid care of the sash. It hung high above the dirty clothes on the carpet of her bedroom and far from the candy wrappers on the floorboard of her small carriage. But, alas, a year is a lengthy time in the life of a teenage girl, and soon my young offspring grew tired of caring for the sash.

I first noticed the problem when the sash appeared in the laundry room atop a mound of dirty clothes. Too soon afterward, I fretted when it reappeared at the bottom of an overstuffed book bag. But when it disappeared for days, I decided that I—and

I alone—must save The Queen. That is when I, the queen mother, also became the keeper of the sash. Whenever Her Highness would yell, "Mom! Where's my sash?", I would make a quick dash in search of the missing sash and, without fail, place it in The Queen's anxious hands.

"Big mistake," my husband, the Queen Daddy, said one morning when he saw me frantically searching for the ribbon. "It's her sash," he lectured. "She needs to take responsibility for it."

"It's a sash," I replied. "How much trouble could it be?"

Without answering, he planted his royal bottom on his reclining throne and shielded his regal scowl with the sports section of the newspaper.

Why does he make such a big deal about a little ol' piece of ribbon? I asked myself, since he obviously was not in the mood for conversation.

The answer to my question did not come until months later, on the final day of The Queen's reign.

The morning began with dark clouds gathering overhead as I chauffeured the queen to her appointments. First, there was a visit to Her Highness's hairdresser, followed by a session with the royal photographer. Between the two destinations, she bawled that her hairdo resembled multiple pigs' tails; it was a curly crisis of queenly magnitude. By the time we arrived for the photo session, her puffy eyes and my twitchy eyes were the only hints of the mother-daughter battle that had ensued moments earlier. We entered the photographer's studio stressed but smiling, for royals must always maintain their decorum in public. A few wardrobe changes for various poses, and we were off again.

After a quick trip home for lunch with the Queen Daddy, we headed back to town for the start of the parade. At the staging area, I dropped off The Queen and then searched for a parking space. Briskly, I walked to the old stone church, where the queen daddy would meet me later. As I sat down on the grassy lawn to rest and recover from the hectic morning, my phone rang.

"Mom! Where's my sash?" Her Highness gasped into a borrowed phone.

My face held a royal flush. "You have it," I said with less certainty than the words implied.

"No, I don't," the queen replied. "And I can't ride without it. Mom, please find it!"

"But where will I find *you* if I do find *it*?" I asked, my mind racing.

The Queen's voice shook. "I don't know! I'm riding in the parade twice—in a convertible and on the float. Please hurry! Oh, Mom, please hurry!"

"Okay!" I promised as a large splat of rain fell on my face.

An adrenaline rush of regal proportions carried me back to the carriage, where, alas, I found no sash.

With trembling fingers, I called the Queen Daddy, who already was headed to the parade in his own carriage. "Go home!" I ordered. "We left her sash!"

"She left it, so she can ride without it!" he ordered back.

"The director of the parade won't let her!" I shouted. "You have to help!" The increased intensity of the rain had magnified the intensity of my voice.

"Grrrrr!" the Queen Daddy growled and hung up, leaving me grateful that he had not spewed the rest of the words into my ear.

As I pondered what I should do next, again my phone rang.

"Mom! I left it at the studio!"

"Are you sure?"

"No, but maybe I did!"

The Queen's fairy tale reign was turning into my worst nightmare.

"Is the photographer still there?" I cried.

"No, he's riding in the parade."

My voice cracked as I thought about the length of the procession. "Wh-where in the parade?"

Over the sound of tuning band instruments, The Queen shouted, "In a car at the front of the line!"

"*Argh!*" I moaned as the clouds exploded like water balloons.

Gritting my teeth, again I was on the run. Wildly, I sped away from my parked car and toward the front of the line. Spying the photographer, I knocked on the windshield and smiled an embarrassed smile.

Lowering the window slightly, he held up a piece of plastic at an angle to shield himself from the torrential rain coming through the opening. Staring at my wilted form, he announced dryly, "You're getting wet."

Ignoring his comment, I leaned my dripping face toward his and said, "My daughter's sash is at your studio."

He shook his head as if he, too, had personal experience with teenage forgetfulness. Then, handing me a ring of keys, he ordered, "Remember to lock it back up." Quickly, he pulled in the scrap of plastic and rolled his window shut.

While others sought shelter from the downpour, I sped through gushing flash floods, my efforts impeded only by the power of the currents.

Back inside the carriage, I shook off water like a peasant's dog and raced out of the parking lot, but soon sat trapped in traffic. Again my phone rang.

"It's not here," the Queen Daddy's voice yelled.

Oops! With the newly acquired information regarding the photographer's studio, I'd totally forgotten about the Queen Daddy.

"I think I know where it is," I told him. "Come back to town and meet me at the old stone church."

"*Grrrr!*" said the Queen Daddy. "You sent me all the way home in this cloudburst and traffic—for nothing?"

I sighed. "You could bring me some dry clothes," I suggested meekly.

The next excruciating, precious minutes ticked away as I sat in stalled traffic and listened to the sound of my own rapid breathing. *Stay calm. Stay calm*, I told myself over and over.

After what seemed like an eternity, the carriages slowly began to move, and at the very same time, the clouds' water assault on the kingdom was coming to an end. Could it be that our luck was changing? My mouth quivered as I dared to hope for a happy ending.

Inside the studio, I found the precious sash. "Yes!" I shouted and jerked the ribbon up and down in a quick celebratory dance. Now, all I needed to do was place it in my daughter's hands.

Although no policeman witnessed the lightning speed of my return trip, one policeman did halt my progress before I could reach my destination. "Sorry, ma'am," he said politely. "Traffic is blocked for the parade."

I had made it this far; I wouldn't give up now. "I need to give something to my daughter!" The volume of my voice competed with a squealing child nearby.

Pointing to a distant parking lot, the policeman firmly suggested, "Park over there and walk." He obviously did not recognize royalty when he saw it.

Too exhausted to challenge his authority, I nodded meekly and did as I was told. Then, grabbing the prized sash, I again was on the run. I zipped across streets and down sidewalks. I squished through mud puddles in a children's park and raced across the lawn of a school.

"I can see the headline in tomorrow's paper," I spoke loudly to my own ears as I maintained the pace. "'Queen's Mother Collapses in Marathon Run Before Parade Begins.'" Then a question came to my lips, "Why? Why are you putting yourself through this?"

There was no time to formulate a rational excuse for a mom gone wild, for at that moment I spied one of my daughter's friends. Skipping a friendly salutation, I instead gasped, "Where is she?" I held up the sash so she would understand the crisis at hand.

Pointing toward a distant speck, the girl answered, "On her float."

"Thank you," I panted.

I sprinted toward the far end of the parade, past high school bands and decorative floats and dancing clowns and noisy fire trucks. I ran past nervous horses and aging veterans and perky cheerleaders and tiny tap dancers. Finally, I made my way to The Queen's float; alas—and unbelievably—there was no queen.

"Where's The Queen?" I coughed out.

"She's at the front in the convertible," answered a young woman standing on the float waiting to join the parade.

Bent over, I gulped air and remembered words spoken months earlier. "Big mistake," the Queen Daddy had said. "It's her sash. She needs to take responsibility for it."

Sighing loudly, I pointed my waterlogged sandals in the opposite direction and sped off. Again, but in reverse order, I sped past tiny tap dancers, aging veterans, nervous horses, and all the other participants until I finally made my way to the front, but the queen was nowhere to be seen!

Standing still for the first time in a long time, I had run out of places to run. Tears poured down my face, for, despite my best efforts, I had failed to save The Queen. In the midst of this personal and public emotional meltdown, I heard a faint, sweet sound that began to grow louder as it approached: it was the anxious voice of a young woman.

"Mom! Mom!" she called.

Quickly, I turned and saw my galloping daughter. Laughing and crying at the same time, I lifted high the sash.

"I love you!" The Queen cried as she spun my exhausted form around with a gigantic hug.

"Greater love hath no other than a mother as she lay down her life for her daughter," I replied (or at least I should have). Actually, I think I said, "I'm having a heart attack."

"What?" The Queen asked.

"Never mind," I sighed. "I love you, too."

Standing to the side of the convertible, I watched as my beautiful, dry daughter slid onto the back seat, then I surveyed the contrast of my own damp and sweaty form.

Again my phone rang.

"I don't see you!" a testy male voice growled. "I'm at the stone church but guess who's not?"

Oh, yes! The Queen Daddy! "Meet me at the bank on King Street. It's closer to where I am right now, and the parade is already starting," I instructed.

The Queen Daddy expressed his extreme displeasure by disconnecting the call.

Once more I was on the run, but when I arrived at the bank on Church Street, the Queen Daddy was not there!

"Oh, no!" I shouted at myself. "I told him to go to the bank on the wrong street!" The rain and stress had melted my brain.

When I could not reach him by phone, I summoned my last ounce of energy and dove into the sea of people, where I bobbed and searched for the Queen Daddy.

Again my phone rang. "Tell me where you are right now and stay still until I find you!" he shouted.

I dared not argue. Standing still as a palace statue, I waited for the Queen Daddy to appear.

It was a less than joyous reunion but a reunion nonetheless. Hand in tightly squeezed hand, we stood as a royal couple and watched The Queen, on her float, make her final passage down the street. Smiling and waving from the throne, Her Highness was charming indeed. People in the crowd told their children, "Look! There's The Queen!"—for they knew her by the crisp, white sash she wore.

Laying my wilted coiffure and mascara-streaked cheek against the Queen Daddy's shoulder, I breathed a royal sigh of relief.

Taking pity on me, the Queen Daddy spoke for the first time that day without growling. "Did you learn something the hard way today?" he asked.

I yawned and replied, "I'll answer that question after I shower and take a nap."

"Then I will wait for your answer," he said.

As the merriment of the festival crowd continued, the two of us slipped quietly away. And we all lived much happier ever after.

—Joan McClure Beck

In Search of the
Perfect Meringue

Marriage. Motherhood. Meringue. Otherwise known as The Sweetest Things in a Woman's Life. At least to my mother, who's spent most of her life perfecting the art of this holy triumvirate. And the rest of it bemoaning my failure to master any of it.

It started with marriage. My mother comes from the Fifties School of Life, which teaches that finding the right mate is the most important decision a woman can make in her life. My mother married my father in 1954. They've been as happy as clams ever since.

Naturally, I got it all wrong. My first husband left me broke with two small children, no college degree, no work experience, and no job prospects. My second husband left me broke with one small child, two teenagers, a roofless house, two dogs, and a small fortune in unpaid taxes. Not to mention a custody battle that cost me my life savings and several months of my life. Did I mention the custody battle that cost me my life savings and several months of my life?

"We never really had any trouble until you started getting married."

My mother is in my kitchen, up to her elbows in eggs and sugar and baking utensils that get used, uh, once a year. She and my father are here on one of their annual trips East from Las Vegas—which my father spends outside on the dock fishing in the lake and my mother spends baking countless pies, cakes, and cookies for our sweets-starved household.

"That's not true." I watch as she separates the egg whites with the spare efficiency of a swordsman. "That can't possibly be true."

She ignores me as she slips the bowl of egg whites into the microwave. "The trick to a good meringue foam is temperature. The egg whites must be at room temperature—not too hot or too cold—before you beat them. If you take the eggs right out of the fridge, you'll need to warm them up a bit first."

Mom has to be wrong. There must be *something* that caused more trouble for my folks than my unfortunate marital alliances.

"What about the war in Vietnam?" I smile, triumphant. Dad spent a tour over there during some of the fiercest fighting of the conflict. A lot of sleepless nights for us all until he came back home safe and sound. "Now *that* was trouble. *Big* trouble."

"It didn't last as long," she says without missing a beat as she pulls the bowl out of the beeping microwave and places it on the counter.

She had me there. I sigh. "I guess not."

Armed now with a wire whisk, my mother whips the egg whites with a surprisingly strong seventy-year-old arm.

"Look, Mom, I didn't *mean* to cause you and Dad any trouble." I watch as the egg whites double and redouble under her capable strokes in mounting folds of rich goo.

"Well, of course you didn't!" Mom whips harder. "It wasn't *your* fault!" She whips furiously now, agitated, and the egg whites stand at full attention in tall peaks rising out of the bowl.

"*You* were never any trouble." She adds the sugar and whips again, attacking the foam. "It was those . . . those . . . those *husbands* of yours."

Overcome, my mother stops short. The whisk in her hand slips and sloppy tufts of meringue soar through the air, landing mostly on my cheeks and chin. She stares at me. "Oh, honey, I'm so sorry!"

I laugh. "Look who's trouble now, Mom."

Mom laughs, too, once she's satisfied that she hasn't blinded me with the makings of her favorite dessert. She puts the whisk down on the counter and dabs at my face with the wet end of a dish towel.

"I'm fine, Mom." I laugh again. "Back to the meringues."

"Of course. Before the foam falls." Mom rushes back to the bowl and spoons the meringue onto the cookie sheet in perfectly formed swirling dollops of spun-sugared bliss.

"Were they really so bad?"

I answer my own question. "Yeah, I guess they were."

"They were *intense*." My mother gives me one of her trademark *I love you but don't understand you* looks. "You've always fallen for intense men. Not good for the long haul."

I think about this while I dip my finger in the bowl and lick up the leftover foam. "That's true. I never really thought about it that way."

"I would have killed them both," my mother says with such force that it occurs to me that she may be a little intense herself.

"It's okay, Mom. The kids are great. I mean they're not perfect, but—"

"My grandchildren are wonderful. But that has nothing to do with their fathers."

"What matters is that they turned out fine, Mom. The rest is ancient history."

"No, it's not. You raised those kids all on your own." Mom shakes her head as she preheats the oven to 250 degrees. "And you're still doing it. You're still doing everything on your own."

In Mom's world, men are men and women do not do anything on their own, except shop. Their men pay the bills, discipline the children, and change the oil in the car every 3,000 miles. The women keep perfect homes, raise perfect children, and make perfect meringues. If they work outside the home, it's because they want to—not because the bank has foreclosed on the house.

"Maybe I'm supposed to, Mom. Maybe my lesson this lifetime is to figure out how to do things on my own."

"Hmmph!" Mom rolls her eyes at me. "Oh, please!"

I don't know what annoys her more, the fact that I could believe such a thing or the New-Age psycho-babble I use to express it. I'm sure that it's a toss-up.

She slaps the rest of the meringues into place on the cookie sheet and pops it into the oven. "A woman needs a man around—just like a man needs a woman." Mom slams the door shut—and I shudder on behalf of the unbaked meringues inside. "If you could just meet the right man . . ."

"A non-intense man?" I tease her at my own risk.

"Yes." My mother raises one of her perfect Elizabeth Taylor eyebrows. "A non-intense man. Like Pergola Man."

Pergola Man is family code for Joel, the man Mom thinks I should have married—but didn't.

"We're just friends, now, Mom, you know that."

The truth is that I broke his heart when I reconciled with my ex—a reconciliation that, of course, did not last—and Joel's never quite trusted me with it again.

"No man builds a woman a pergola unless he's in love with her." Mom sets the oven timer for an hour. She points to the sink. "You wash, I'll dry."

This is family code for I have something to say and you're going to listen. We wash up; Mom talks—and I listen.

"A good relationship is like a good meringue," she says. "None of this intense, crazy love stuff that burns out in a flash. You need to start at room temperature and warm up as you go. You set the oven on low, and over a slow heat the meringue sets."

"That's lovely, Mom." I grin at her. "But I never did learn to make a decent meringue."

"You had your first lesson today. I hope you were paying attention."

Dishes done, Mom throws the towel at me to dry my hands. "I took the liberty of inviting Pergola Man over for dinner. He should be here in an hour."

"I see. Just about the time the meringues are coming out of the oven." My mother is nothing if not subtle.

"Exactly." My mother gives me a quick hug. "There's not a man alive who can resist a good meringue."

Any more than I can resist my mother.

—*Paula Munier*

A Nonstandard Mother

Every school morning, for just a few moments, my world kaleidoscopes to a different reality. I stand on the curb in front of our blue, Cape Cod–style tract house and watch my eighteen-year-old daughter, Sophie, buckle her seatbelt. Sofe looks at me out the window of the yellow, special education school bus, and it begins. I wave in an odd square pattern, and she copies me. I throw her a kiss, and she throws one back. By then, the bus has taken off and I pretend to run after it. Sophie can see me through the back window. I wave in a climbing pattern and dance around. As she copies my motions back to me, I can see her fading form move farther and farther away. Only after the bus has turned the corner of our block do I notice that I am standing in the middle of the street. I walk back across my neat front lawn, back into my kitchen to my hot cup of coffee. And my status changes. Now, not only could I pass for someone with no children, I could also pass for someone with no disabled child.

Life seems luxurious, silent. As I sip, I think about how, because of my daughter's chromosomal anomaly, Down syndrome, she has been part of this gang of kids on the bus for several years. Paul, who has mild cerebral palsy, is tall now and handsome. He bowls with Sophie after school. Red-headed Dennis is the talkative leader of the pack; he has multiple congenital disabilities, including limited use of one arm. Once, he broke his good arm and was very convivial, explaining when I had brought donuts for a school party that I would have to feed him his. I laughed and said, "Nice try, Den," and placed the glazed dessert in his casted fingers. He had to lean toward his hand, but he did very well on his own. And there's Diana—tall, blond, funny, and a fashion plate. She has a mystery diagnosis of delay accompanied by the resulting anger and frustration that makes her life more complicated than it should have been. When she comes to visit Sophie for any extended amount of time, her mom gives me a neatly labeled zip-locked plastic bag containing a colorful medley of medications.

When I am not with Sophie and am passing as a standard parent, sometimes I see a family with a child with a disability. I invariably have an urge to come out of the closet. It is not sentimentality about the disability that draws me. Disabilities just make things hard to do. But disabilities remind me of my daughter. I want to stop and say, "I recognize you. I'm only pretending to be a standard mother. And your family reminds me of someone I love."

My first strong experience of passing as a standard mother occurred when Sofe was twelve and went away to Girl Scout camp for a weekend. Toothbrush, pajamas, bathing suit, bandana, mess kit, sit-upon, and official Girl Scout flashlight were all packed neatly in her pink you-pull-it suitcase. After she proudly pulled the suitcase herself to her barracks-style cabin, I made a little bed for her from the soft blanket and rose-patterned sheets we had brought along. I had an image of Baby Bear's bed in the woods as I stepped back to admire my handiwork.

"Sophie may need a little assistance and attention," I mentioned quietly to her camp counselor as my daughter was exploring what were to be her new surroundings for the next three days.

"Oh, she'll have plenty of fun! Don't worry about a thing," the counselor reassured me.

"Well, even though she doesn't have accidents, she may need to be reminded to use the restroom," I added. Sophie was the only Girl Scout with a disability at the camp.

"All the girls are reminded, in the morning, before and after meals. No problem," the counselor answered kindly, tolerating me.

As Sophie's father and her two brothers, Max and Moe, were hugging Sophie goodbye, I was proud of myself that I didn't also tell the counselor, "You don't understand . . . see, she's a goddess and must be cared for at all times. What if she can't find her stuff in her suitcase, and what if she puts her shoes on the wrong feet? Will you ask her to change them in a way that doesn't embarrass her in front of the other girls? And make sure she uses a napkin at meals. And she's a good swimmer, but watch her anyway. And listen to everything she says. And make sure she makes a friend and that someone hugs her at least once a day."

I also confess that, when we all got back into the car and I realized Sofe was safe and would be engaged for the entire camp visit, I felt this wave of relief so intense it was as if something had flown out of me into the far sky.

There were just the four of us in the car, not the eternal five. I had a fleeting thought of how weird it was not to have Sophie, since, due to her lack of a regular social life, she was with us so much of the time. All the time, really. There were few birthday party invitations, few play dates away, no overnights.

But then, another thought entered my head. It was a guilty one. It was the thought that we could pass now. I could pretend we were a family with no disability. I could act just like every other mother, with no one staring surreptitiously at her child and her in the mall. I could act like a mother with just toothaches, science projects, and knee scratches to handle.

I was so used to my own silent fight, the set of my jaw, my pride, my quick smile to cover the hurt, my constant vigilance, my concern for my daughter's well-being. I was surprised how deflated I felt without it. I was surprised how elated I felt without it.

As I sit in my kitchen after seeing Sophie off to school, I know that these feelings have not changed much.

Even though families like mine are isolated in ways, I would not campaign for a larger member base. This is probably not a club any of us would have volunteered to join. But I'm in. And whenever I am not with my child, I am only pretending that I am not a lifetime member—bound to, confounded by, and in love with this heartbreaking, heart-mending, exquisite experience that is motherhood. Surrounded by the confusion and ecstasy that is my own unique version of this adventure, I realize I can never really pass. Because my heart is forever formed by what is real: a nonstandard child, a nonstandard motherhood, and what is now my standard and extraordinary life.

—*Jolie Kanat*

It Never Ends

It's 9:00 A.M. and I'm already tired. I'm fixing my five-year-old, Rose, her lunch. Tough stuff. She doesn't like sandwiches.

"Just a blob of peanut butter, Mom" she announces decisively. She's industriously working on her letters.

I fix the blob of peanut butter, add a piece of oat nut bread, milk in Ariel's thermos, a banana, and I'm done.

"How was your breakfast, honey," I ask, looking at the clock.

"Delicious, Mom! My tummy is doing a parade for you!"

I stop dead in my tracks. "Your tummy is doing a parade for me?"

"Uh huh," she answers matter-of-factly, blissfully unaware of her obvious incredible budding poetic genius.

"Ow!" My one-year-old bites me. Hard. On the thigh. It hurts. A lot. "No, Ruby, no! Don't bite me!"

"Mom! Those are bad words," the five-year-old admonishes me. "Don't yell at a baby! She doesn't know any better!" Her voice sounds superior, condescending, and familiar.

"I'm not yelling," I defend myself, rubbing my thigh. "I'm speaking firmly so she knows I'm serious."

"Ow!" The baby bites again. "Goddammit, Ruby!"

"Mom! Those are bad words!"

I check my thigh, my mind racing. *Is the skin broken? Do I need a shot? Is this any indication of her future activities? Why does she look so gleeful when she bites?*

I open a cabinet and pull out Tupperware. The one-year-old goes for it.

"Look, Mom. I wrote my first word. I sounded it out." The five-year-old proudly holds up her work. Clearly and crookedly, the letters are displayed: V G Y N.

I try to look pleased and excited, not shocked and dismayed. "Wow," I say. "Almost perfect. Isn't there another word you would like to write? There are so many."

"Nope," she says. "Did I get it right? What are the letters?" She looks so eager with her pencil poised.

I tell her. "V A G—"

"You're going too fast!" she says.

"I . . . N . . . A."

The one-year-old has tired of the Tupperware and is looking for trouble.

It's 9:05. I have ten minutes to get teeth brushed, hair combed, show-and-tell decided, shoes and jackets on, and a path cleared to the door. Doable.

My stomach grumbles. As I grab my shopping list, checkbook, and baby, I toss a piece of bread into the temperamental toaster oven. I herd the five-year-old into the bathroom, passing my girlfriend's new baby gift on the dining room table, where it has been sitting for a week. Another reminder of another undone errand.

The toothbrush is crusty from not being rinsed properly. The bath towels are still damp on the floor from last night's bath. I forgot to straighten up the bathroom, I realize, as I remember crashing before around 9:30 the night before. Pathetic.

"Can I wear some makeup, Mommy?"

"No!"

"How about some lipstick?"

"No!"

"Perfume?"

"Hey, knock it off!" I say. "Please."

"Well then, how about some earrings?"

"Rose! For God's sake!"

She's five years old and born to accessorize. We have these little fashion chitchats about 500 times a day! Drives me crazy!

She attempts a lengthy monologue about outfits and makeup.

"Brush your teeth," I very firmly tell her, trying to keep the one-year-old out of the toilet, the bath, the cabinets. "Hurry up—please, Rose."

I'm losing it. It's 9:10. Always rushing.

We head back to the bedroom for the hair-brushing experience, where we argue about clips and bows, colors and size, placement and quantity.

Rose stops suddenly. "Mom, how many pecks *did* Peter Piper pick?"

I look at her in astonishment. How does she come up with this stuff? I start to laugh. Hard. Really hard. Tears stream down my face. They both stare at me.

"It's just tension," I say as my laughter turns into sobs.

"What's tension?" asks my now clearly concerned five-year-old.

I think. "It's what Cinderella felt when the clock chimed at midnight and she had to get back to the coach."

"Oh," she nods understandingly.

I sigh, wipe my face. My breakdown is over.

I've been up since 5:45 and have showered, dressed, changed three diapers, straightened two bedrooms, fixed two breakfasts, blow-dried my hair (always a challenge and a luxury), emptied the dishwasher, scrubbed the stove, fixed a pot of coffee, read some of the newspaper, changed over the water dispenser, administered eye drops, talked to my mother (or rather listened to her), swept the kitchen floor, taken out the garbage, arranged a play date, taught two important life lessons, put in a load of laundry, cuddled my kids, and had a meaningful conversation in gibberish.

I miss my girlfriends and brunch, my soft hands and pre-pregnancy bladder. I miss peeing in peace and showering languidly. But mostly, I miss my husband. He's been on a business trip for nine days. I don't know how single mothers do it.

"Hey, Mom, what's that smell?"

The ever-observant five-year-old snaps me out of my reverie. The toast is burning. Quickly, before the smoke alarm goes off and traumatizes the one-year-old, I leap into the kitchen, unplug the toaster, swat at the smoking toast, toss it into the sink, open the kitchen window and the sliding glass door. The girls, sensing excitement, run and giggle.

"Oh, Mom, you poor thing! What about your breakfast?"

I grab a banana. The one-year-old shrieks madly, her usual reaction to the sight of food.

"Okay, okay," I tell her, breaking off half of the banana.

She grabs it and shoves it in her mouth. She giggles adorably, cheeks bulging banana.

"Mom, Ruby's manners are ferocious!" Rose giggles wildly and careens off into the bedroom.

"You mean atrocious, and please get your shoes on—the maroon ones, and no argument or no TV for a week!"

Am I crazy? No TV for a week? I pray she obeys so I don't have to make good on my threat.

She says, incredibly, "Okay, Mom."

I put the baby in the car seat, strap her in, go back in the house, get my purse and Rose's lunch pail, deposit them in the car, and return to the house.

"Rose! Whatchadoin? Let's GO!"

It's now 9:35. The five-year-old is in my bedroom. I hear her talking. I peek in. She's in front of my full-length mirror pretending to apply makeup.

"Who are you talking to," I ask her, brush in hand, leading her into the kitchen where Ruby can see us from the car.

"Rosieanna," she answers. Rosieanna, her imaginary friend in the mirror that she's had since she was three years old. Rosieanna, who always tells her to do bad stuff. Rosieanna, who always gets the blame for everything. Rosieanna, who is always wearing my clothes!

The hair is brushed; the hell with show and tell. I get the five-year-old in the car and buckle her in. She's chattering nonstop, as usual, about some outfit in her future. I shut the door and hear her muffled monologue as I go back inside, survey the damage, hit the security alarm, and get out of the house. Open the gate, get in the car.

Ruby is contentedly sucking on her pacifier. Rose is actually quiet, looking at a book. I get in my seat, buckle up, turn on the car, turn off the radio, and put my head back. Silence. Real, honest-to-God silence. *Ahhhhh.*

I take out my lipstick and look in the mirror. As I begin to apply it, my eyes catch Rose's in the mirror.

"Mom, please, oh please, oh please, can I have some lipstick?"

"No!"

"Please! Just a little?"

"No, no, no!"

"How about a lipstick kiss, then, Mom—pleeeeeeze?"

It never ends.

—*Amy Simon*

Missing . . . You

I did it again. I devoured another day on the Internet searching for her. I see her picture daily, on my bedroom wall. It's my only material clue to the mystery of the woman in the photograph. She is an enigma to me. But I know she loved me.

As I write this, I realize that my words may appear small, inconsequential, as I attempt to puzzle out the scant details I know of her life. I wonder if I have the right.

The woman on my wall is my birth mother.

How do I know she loved me? I know because, when my older brother, sister, and I were taken away from her after she threw us all out in the middle of the night forty-one years ago, I listened to her cries fade in the darkness as we sped away in my father's station wagon, steam spreading on the rear window, our noses pressed against the glass. "Nooo! . . . Come back! . . ." her voice carried through the night air. Silently, I watched her grow smaller as she ran down the street, chasing the red tail lights of my dad's Country Squire, until no matter how hard I searched in the streetlights for a glimmer of her nightgown-clad figure, she was gone. I was seven.

After the Second World War, much of the United States prospered. Men wore white shirts and fedoras, and women wore dresses even when they spent four hours of their day in the kitchen. Television was making its big debut along with its somewhat dubious companion, the TV dinner. The best time for Linda Lou Cain, my mother, would have been during that period, the fifties. She was in her teens. She would have had Elvis as her rebel icon and a hula-hoop to wile away the hot summer days. As a growing girl, she probably ate dozens of eggs, thick slices of bacon, and hundreds of peanut butter and jelly sandwiches. There would have been bottles of ice-cold whole milk to wash it all down. For dinner, she most likely ate roast beef, mashed potatoes with gravy, and buttered green beans.

I know her parents weren't poor because my sister has a photograph of her father standing next to a modest-sized fishing boat wearing his white captain's hat and a navy blue pea coat. I know he traveled, liked deep sea fishing, and collected carved wooden animals in miniature. Her grandfather, Frank C. Cain, was mayor of Cleveland Heights, Ohio, for a record-breaking thirty-two years, and Cain Park is aptly named after her family.

I vaguely remember visiting my grandparents in a nice house on Compton Avenue, with nice furniture and no uninvited guests, like the gluttonous, slimy gray rat that had taken up residence in our own home. What was it eating, anyway?

In her youth, I suppose my mother wore gloves on blustery winter days and had learned such womanly things as applying lipstick and rouge and how to hem a poodle skirt. Looking back, I believe she had all she needed. But as her child, I knew nothing of any of this, nor did I care. Because ten years later on East Scarborough in the era of peace and love, nobody knew that I was always hungry, had rarely worn gloves in the winter, and once had a sizable clump of my hair lopped off by a neighbor girl who took the scissors to the tangled mass that was stuck fast to a wad of Bazooka bubble gum, and finally, nobody knew that I was growing up backward instead of forward. No one knew that life in the Yellow Submarine, as we called our house, was far less hospitable than the cheery rendition of the Beatles' song. The cupboards and refrigerator inside were bare, and I recall salivating over a single box of Pop-Tarts I once saw amid the clutter on my mother's dresser.

Maybe you can tell by now that I have a fixation with food. When my siblings and I lived with our mother, there was little of it. It is no small miracle that today I am not as wide around as I am tall.

As a mother thirty years later, I filled my son's plate edge to edge every night for dinner. He often grumbled about this. Invariably, he ate only what he wanted, which was just fine. Some of the best days when I was raising him were when the mortgage was paid and I had just been to the grocery store. The refrigerator and cupboards were stocked with cereal, macaroni and cheese, jars of spaghetti sauce, bottles of juice, rolls of kielbasa, cans of tuna, the occasional roast, plenty of milk, fixings for chicken noodle soup, and of course, strawberry Pop-Tarts.

I have only snapshots and a handful of faded memories about life with my mother. I remember having awful leg aches and somehow ending up in her bed and her telling me to push my leg hard into the footboard because somehow it would help to ease the pain.

She never seemed to sleep but rarely got out of bed. The bed I slept in while living in the Yellow Submarine was four mattresses high. Why, you ask? I have no idea. All I do know is when I wanted down I needed help. Once, I remember falling out of that padded plateau onto the hard wooden floor with a resounding thud, followed by my ensuing "Agggghh-hhhh." Years later, I read "The Princess and the Pea" and had one of those aha moments. I suspect, however, my elevated sleeping conditions had nothing to do with testing my delicate skin for royal bloodlines.

I was perhaps five when I heard a particular song on the radio. I know today it was "MacArthur Park." I remember my mother standing in the upstairs hallway framed by the yellow backlight from her bedroom as the song played. She was crying. I wanted to ask her what was wrong, why she'd come undone by those strange lyrics about "sweet green icing flowing down" and someone leaving "cake out in the rain." I was all about the cake; she wept long black lines of mascara. I wondered why the song made her so sad but couldn't pry the question from my lips.

Those scant memories are wed to the amygdala portion of my brain—the part that is the primary processor of memory and emotional reactions. I'm left with thoughts of sadness and unanswered questions about that period of my life and about my mother, both of which I've spent much time mulling over. Why, for example, had my mother's life shrunken to the span of a thirteen-by-twelve-foot bedroom? Did she really grow up normal as I've imagined? Did she like peanut butter, hate homework, and have crushes on boys other than Elvis? What sorts of books did she read? Did she graduate from high school? What was her favorite color, and did she have any artistic inclinations, as I do? Was she an idealist, or had she abandoned all hope before she even developed breasts?

The picture on my wall gives up nothing of the chaotic, drug-dependant woman who threw us out of the house in the middle of the night all those years ago. It reveals none of her private struggles and most desperate moments. It is serene, in fact. The black and white portrait is soft. There is a hint of a smile on her full lips. Her dark brown eyes beneath heavy brows were clear and untroubled. Her skin was pale and unmarked, and she had all her teeth. She must have been in her late teens or early twenties. Grace Kelly had nothing on her.

I know that picture was taken before my parents' divorce, when I was two, before the antidepressants, before my mother's inability to care for us, before her eventual landslide into addiction with street narcotics and bad men. And long before her manic depression swallowed her up until she was no longer even a blip on the radar screen.

Why dredge up those unhappy memories, you might ask? Where's the happily ever after? What are these words of tattered memories and unrequited wonderings doing in a book honoring and celebrating mothers? This is not motherhood, you might declare—it's an abomination. Mothers don't leave.

While all that may be so, my mother has never left me. She continues to exist in my heart and my mind. And her failures are not all there was to my mother; they are not all she was, and remains, to me. Hindsight tells me that you don't know what someone else's life is really like unless you live it. I was compelled to see the larger picture. Now, as I speak softly of her life, I only want her to know that I don't hold her in ill regard.

I had a counselor tell me years ago that you do the best you can with the tools you have at the time. I know motherhood is hard. I had to do it on my own, as a single mother and without a mother to model or to help. I faced my own tremendous obstacles. At first, I worried that child abuse was cyclical and that I'd follow in the same footsteps, but I underestimated my love for my son and how much I wanted to protect him. No, I didn't make the same mistakes my mother had. I wasn't the perfect mother, though, and with perfect hindsight, I see where I could've done better.

One of my last memories of my mother is of an incident that happened when I was about six. I was doing something I wasn't supposed to (again). We were all outside in the afternoon—I and every other kid on the street—and a tornado was coming. I remember the absolute stillness and how the sky and everything around us slowly began to turn yellow. There was not a sound but our excited chatter and then the rush of the wind through the trees as the sky above began to cook.

When all hell broke loose, we scattered like the leaves and debris that began flying through the air. I ended up in the middle of the street in front of our house, scared out of my socks, as the noise and chaos erupted around me. Day turned to night, and the air was thick with the sound of the wind roaring like a steam engine thundering down the tracks. As the twister bore down on us, I swear to this day that my feet began to leave the ground, and out of the darkness shot a hand that latched on to my arm like a pair of vise grips and pulled me back down. It was my mother.

I found out later that she sprained both ankles trying to get to me.

It didn't take stormy weather for me to bond with my son and do everything in my power to keep him safe and well. And he was never hungry—for food or anything else. Not a day went by that I didn't tell him, and show him, that I loved him. We had our burger and movie nights. I played baseball with him in the front yard and was the first to put a basketball in his hand. We played weeklong games of Monopoly, and he helped me with my logic homework when I was in college. I cooked his favorite birthday dinners and didn't force him to eat suspicious stalk-like vegetables that needed to be covered with hollandaise sauce. When I drove him to college, I cried most of the way home—but they were mostly tears of joy and pride for him.

Even though I am a much different mother than my mother was, I understand that part of who I am today is part of who I was when I was living with her. There is still a bit of that child in me. But it didn't dictate how I lived my life or how I raised my son.

Still, it has been difficult living a life of wondering. Did I inherit my clear skin from her? Was she introspective like me? Did she play with dolls or roast potato bugs with a magnifying glass in the hot summer sun?

Most of all, it has been difficult living a life completely devoid of her presence. We never shared confidences or our dreams. We never exchanged our favorite book titles or cooking recipes. Regrettably, she never got to meet my son. We never fought. We never got it right or wrong. There were never classic battles or rifts or misunderstandings to overcome. She was just . . . missing.

How many of us get do-overs, you might ask? Not many, it's true.

I have to tell you, though, that if her hand shot out of the darkness seeking my own once again, I would take it. I would bring her back, give her that second chance. Not that I'd expect a happy ending; I know life isn't always that nice and tidy. But I never got to tell my mother that part of me still loves her, that I understand her failures. So, with these words, I just wanted to say that, while she wasn't perfect, she was my mother. And I've missed her. And failure isn't always as it appears.

—Elizabeth Klanac

Stir-Fry Love

I reach for a worn handle. The tapered wood, one inch in diameter at its thickest point, slips between my fingers like a key in its lock. A warm feeling shoots into my hand, different from the flames heating the well-seasoned wok before me. I wonder how many times Mom had gripped the handle of this wok? How many hours had she stood over it waiting for the oil to get that wavy look before tossing in meats and vegetables expertly sliced and diced by her hands.

I turn to cut some ginger, and with a sweep of my knife's blade, I scoop slivers of the flavorful root into the wok. The ginger hits the oil and sizzles immediately but not so much that it burns. I inhale the familiar smell and sigh—and I'm no longer a grown and married man with a child on the way.

I'm eight years old and taking my turn on the front of a shopping cart. Mom weaves in and out of the grocery aisle, ignoring the wobbling front wheel and shooting down my requests for sugar-laden cereals. The mountain of food in the cart dwarfs my mother's five-foot frame. She squints at a handwritten list with the same scrutiny as an accountant reviewing a financial statement. A dozen or so coupons attempt an escape out of her purse but fail, as she stuffs them back in and closes the zipper. Getting the most bang for the buck is essential with three kids and Dad's single income, but Mom is a master in this game of raising a healthy family, and no master skimps on food.

We pass the deli and take a number. Customers shift back and forth, impatiently checking their numbers and the "Now Serving" monitor. We will not wait; Mom has a plan. We're number 88; plenty of time to hit the produce department and come back.

We stop at the cherries. Mounds of the deep red fruit are piled high. Some are still cold, and condensation covers the freshest ones. Pits are scattered along the front edge of the display. I add to the slipping hazard by taste testing and launching a couple pits of my own. Mom instructs me not to eat too many because they are not washed. For every one she sees me eat, I eat two behind her back. Other customers stuff handfuls into their bags, but not Mom. Each cherry is handpicked by her careful eye; the tender attention adds sweetness.

Back at home, she washes the cherries and sets them out for our eager fingers. Strawberries are next, but first she cores each one with a paring knife. Every single strawberry is cradled momentarily while the knife, seemingly working on its own, twists in a small circle. Soon, a dented and faded aluminum colander in the middle of the counter is filled. I wander over with cherry-stained lips and rest a hand on the edge of the Formica. She pushes the colander closer, turning it to a particular position. I stand on tiptoe and reach and reach. If the colander weren't full, I wouldn't be able to grasp anything. Mom grins like she has a secret. My hand clutches something so large it can't be a strawberry, but it is.

"Wow!" I proclaim.

"That's a big one," she replies as her knife flashes back and forth on the cutting board.

With the fruit and vegetables all washed and cut, she switches to prepping a large piece of beef.

"Cut against the grain of the meat," she instructs. "Makes it more tender."

I watch the marbled meat fall victim to even strokes of the knife. Mom's fingers are safely tucked under her knuckles, and in no time a pile of kid-size pieces sits neatly on the round cutting board. One day I will be allowed to use a knife, and one day I will cut with the same grace. For now, I just eat big strawberries and watch.

The meat goes into a bowl with a handful of green onions, a splash of rice vinegar, sesame oil, and a liberal dousing of soy sauce. Last, she sprinkles some cornstarch over the beef.

"What's that for?" I ask.

"It gives the meat a silky texture. Here, why don't you help Mom stir it all up," she replies, handing me the bowl.

I watch the white powder disappear and congeal onto the meat as I stir and take in the unique aroma of Chinese cuisine.

"That's enough," she says, taking the bowl and placing it on the counter next to the stove. Different colored bowls stand at attention next to the wok. The wok sitting atop the stove with its shiny wooden handle safely out of my reach is ready—ready for the union with my mother's hand and the ingredients of our future meal.

An hour later, the scraping of a metal spatula curls through the house, letting everyone know it's dinnertime. Steam rises over Mom's shoulders and hovers briefly before being sucked into the exhaust.

Her long black hair sways lightly as she stirs in a mixture of cornstarch and broth to thicken the gravy. Finally, she turns and pours the stir-fry into a serving dish. Dinner is served.

Almost thirty years have passed since the initiation of that wok. Now, I have it in my kitchen and grip it with the same love that Mom did. I swirl with the corner of my metal spatula, watching the thickened gravy bubble and cling to every bit of the stir-fry, like good gravy should.

I call my wife, Lori, to dinner, just as the phone rings.

"Hi, Mom." I hold the phone to my ear with my shoulder and empty the wok.

The inevitable question is coming.

"Have you been eating well?" she asks.

I smile and motion for Lori to sit down.

"Yes, Mom."

—*Ryan Chin*

Empty Nest Christmas

My youngest daughter moved out of the house just a few weeks before Christmas; she was the last one of the three to leave the nest. But it was okay. It was time to move on, for both of us. She was ready to assert her independence, and I was ready to make a few changes to the house—a new guest bedroom, for instance. She also had taken her dogs—all three of them—and the house was, indeed, quiet. Ahh, sweet bliss! Visions of long, uninterrupted bubble baths began to emerge.

"Oh, Mom, are you going to be okay?" lamented daughter number two as she helped me unpack the Christmas decorations. "You're going to be all alone when you wake up on Christmas morning."

Pop! There went that bubble of idyllic solitude. I hadn't thought of waking to an empty house on Christmas.

"Are you going to hang your stocking?" she asked.

One December when my three girls were little, I had made all of us Christmas stockings of jewel-toned velvet—in our favorite colors, banded with quilted gold lamé and trimmed with ribbon. Each girl had taken hers when she moved out, and all I had now was my own.

Their father and I had been divorced for about ten years, so I was pretty much used to being alone, I thought. Still, on Christmas morning there had always been stockings filled with candy and small gifts hanging from the mantle. Seeing what was in our stockings had always been one of our favorite traditions. It was often a creative challenge to find things that would actually fit into the stockings.

No, I hadn't thought of a Christmas morning without at least one daughter to share our stocking tradition. Now, when I did, imagining a single, empty stocking hanging from the fireplace seemed awfully lonely.

"Probably not," I answered my middle child. "Thanks a lot, daughter!" I teased.

Several times over the weeks leading up to Christmas, I tried to imagine how I would feel waking up alone on Christmas morning. Finally, I just resigned myself to making do with a mug of hot coffee and a plate of my favorite Christmas cookies. I always baked cookies. This year I had given most of them away to the girls—keeping a few for myself, of course. I would just have to cope.

As it turned out, I hung my stocking after all, deciding it was just a decoration and hoping that someday there would be two stockings hanging side by side—that I would have someone special to make and fill a new stocking for. It looked pretty. A Christmas hearth needed stockings, even if it was only one!

I spent Christmas Eve at my mother's house, where we had our traditional celebration with uncles, aunts, and cousins. That, too, had been changing over time; there were fewer and fewer of us every year. The girls and their boyfriends stopped in, of course. But they all were in serious relationships, which meant they had other stops to make that night. I wasn't the only mother who had to be kept happy on Christmas Eve! It was a nice evening, and we all had a wonderful time. But I guess nothing ever lives up to those memories of Christmas as a kid and when you have children of your own.

It was snowing as I drove home. Winter in Illinois was generally freezing, and the snow was cold, messy, and dangerous to drive in. Arizona in winter was looking better and better, and with my nest now empty, I was beginning to give it some serious consideration.

I hung up my coat, got into my pajamas, and settled into my favorite comfy chair in the living room to bask in the glow of the Christmas lights. It was so peaceful. But what to my wondering eyes should appear! My stocking, hanging from the mantle, was filled to the brim! Shiny bows peeked from the top, a couple more were scattered on the hearth. I could not have been more surprised. *There really is a Santa!* I thought. I laughed, I cried, I shook my head. It was the sweetest thing anyone could have done for me! I couldn't resist. I opened one package and left the rest until morning.

Such fun it was having those gifts to open the next morning! Lovely soaps, bath oil, lotions, and a sea sponge. I would have those bubble baths I'd been dreaming about. There were even a couple of new CDs for me to listen to as I soaked. My daughters made my Christmas that year. Sure, I was their mother, but it was so thoughtful. I felt so proud of them. I assumed they had gotten together and picked a designated stocking stuffer, but I found out later that was not the case. They each had come up with the idea and made the trip on their own, independent of one another.

The neighbors must have wondered at my exuberance as I shoveled the snow from the walk that morning—waving and calling out "Merry Christmas!" My children loved me. And my nest would never be empty of their love. What more could any mother want?

—Mauverneen Blevins

My Mother, Myself

If I said that the last couple of days were challenging for me, it would be a massive understatement. My daughter got sick on Saturday. It started with a sore throat followed by a low-grade fever. On Sunday morning, she threw up the Motrin I had given her for the fever. She slept most of the day. In the afternoon, the fever reached 103 degrees, and I dragged her kicking and screaming to urgent care.

She was miserable, dizzy, and a bit incoherent. She hates throat swabs. Fortunately, we got a wonderful nurse who was gentle with her. The minute the nurse was gone, my daughter threw up all over the exam room. There was no bin or wastebasket for me to put in front of her. I had to hold her up because she was dizzy and hold her hair back while she vomited. The doctor walked into the room to find a scene straight out of a horror movie. They rushed us into another exam room. An antibiotic was prescribed, and we were sent home.

I spent Sunday night sleeping in the living room to be closer to her just in case she needed to get up and became too dizzy to walk. She managed to keep her antibiotic down that night, thank goodness.

By the time Monday morning rolled around, I was pretty much a walking zombie who bore an uncanny resemblance to Medusa. My daughter got up and drank some water—and immediately threw up.

I helped my son get ready for school. While waiting for the bus, he got his bike out of the garage and rode it up and down the sidewalk and driveway. Just before the bus came, his bike hit one of the last remaining patches of ice on the sidewalk and he fell, scraping his knee and ripping the last good pair of jeans he owns. While I cleaned and bandaged his knee and he changed his pants, the bus came and went.

After getting my daughter settled down on the couch, I drove my son to school. Since I had some paperwork to turn in at the school office, I decided to wait for the bell and walk into the school with him. We stood next to a woman who is a recess monitor at the school.

My son, who is one of the most amiable and outgoing kids you will ever find, saw her and said, "Hi, recess monitor!"

An annoyed look crossed her face. "Well, if it isn't Mr. I-Didn't-Do-It," she said with a smirk, looking very proud of herself.

Now, I know my son works hard to cultivate his reputation as a troublemaker. He is not an angel by any stretch of the imagination. But lately I'd noticed that he was being sent to the guidance counselor's office for relatively minor infractions of the rules at school. I volunteer at the school, and I see reports on the other students for far worse offenses, for which they got off with mere warnings. Things were becoming very clear to me as I stood looking at the recess monitor from hell.

I have a temper that I can usually keep in check. But from time to time, it almost seems like there is a "clutch" in my brain that disengages any control my brain has over my mouth. This was one of those times. After taking a second to consider what the repercussions would be if I lambasted this woman, I decided that her smirk and rude tone were my welcome mat to a temporary insanity defense.

With my left hand on my hip and my right index finger pointing, I made searing eye contact with her and said, "Lay off my son." I didn't recognize my own voice. I scared myself.

Then the bell rang. The monitor, who looked as if all the blood had drained from her face, put a protective arm around each of her daughters and hurried them into school.

I told my son to have a good day. His brown eyes looked like they were dancing. He gave me a smile and wave and dashed off to his classroom.

As I reached the school office, I looked up to see the monitor walking down the hallway and looking back over her shoulder at me.

I gave her a look that said, *Yes, I'm still watching you.*

I felt exhausted. It wasn't even 9:00 yet, and I already had been thrown up on, bled on, and had nearly gotten into a smack-down with another woman.

When I got back out to the car, I caught my reflection in the rearview mirror. I saw my mother staring back.

My mother is a roller coaster. You simply never know from minute to minute whether she's going to go along at a leisurely pace or throw you around a curve. Sometimes, you can feel yourself chugging upward just before a freefall. And you're turned upside down quite a bit. But, in all our years together, she has been my biggest defender.

As a little girl with thick glasses and unruly hair, I would get picked on at school. My mother would get in my face and say, "My kids are some of the best people who ever walked the Earth. Now, get out there and stand up for yourself." She simply could not understand why I would ever let other kids intimidate me.

Growing up, I often felt frightened in new situations. Again, my mother could not understand my timidity and would say, "You've got two legs and a mouth, don't you? Use them!"

My mother was, and still is, brash and direct. Patience was never her strong suit. She doesn't have a subtle bone in her body, and she is a force to be reckoned with.

I have a memory of my mom that I treasure. When I was in fourth grade, she bought me ice skates and took a friend and me to a place called Lake Park to skate. The problem was, I had never been on ice skates in my life. I couldn't even stand up. Mom had been watching me from the car. She strode out onto the ice and picked me up. My friend was skating circles around us. Mom pointed at her and said, "Just do what she's doing." Then she lit a cigarette and held it in the air with two fingers of her left hand and her right arm crossed in front of her. It was as though she thought she could make me skate by sheer force of will.

Don't think about things—just do them.

There is a line from one of the Star Wars movies that always reminds me of my Mom. Yoda is teaching Luke Skywalker to be a Jedi, and he says, "Do or do not, there is no try." My mom, the Jedi master. The force is definitely strong in her.

I have so many good childhood memories of my mom. She taught me to embroider. I can still see her taking a dish towel and using a round cap from a pill bottle and a pencil to draw a bunch of grapes for me to embroider. She would buy me paint-by-number kits, and we would paint together for hours. It was Mom who would hold up math flashcards and drill me on them. Later, it was Mom I would call and cry to when things went wrong. And she would always tell me, "You might as well laugh through grief as cry though it."

That's my mom. She always tells it like she sees it, no holds barred. Sometimes her straightforward talk bowls me over, but she always builds me back up.

A few years ago, I wrote my mom a letter on Mother's Day. I typed out all the reasons why I felt she was a wonderful mother. In twenty minutes, I had typed two pages, single-spaced, full of reasons. I mailed it to her. I was so proud of myself. I was sure she would love it.

She called me after she got it. She told me she wanted me to sign it and have it notarized, because she didn't believe I'd written it. But I know she liked it.

If you are looking for hearts and flowers from my mom, you are "barking up the wrong tree," as she would say. Some say that God chooses a mother for each baby born, the one who will give us everything we need. There have been times in my life when my relationship with my mother has made me say, "Lord, what were you thinking?" But now that I am a mother, I am surprised at how wise she's always been. She instilled in me a strong sense of self. Whenever someone tries to knock me down in any way, there is a part of me that is like a punching bag with sand in the bottom of it. It takes the hit and comes back full force.

I feel that, in a strange way, the altercation with the recess monitor has earned me some "Mom stripes." My son knows that I've got his back and that I am a force to be reckoned with. My mother would be proud.

—Jamie Wojcik

A Few Days Off

"Can I steal the girls for a few days?" My sister's babysitting offer hangs in the air for exactly two seconds before my husband jumps all over it. "Sure! We'll drop them off Saturday afternoon. Can we pick them up on Wednesday?"

Wednesday? Four whole days without my five-year-old dashing through the house, leaving a trail of storybooks and doll clothes in her wake? Four whole days free of shuttling my eight-year-old back and forth to the pool, park, and playground?

I start to dream, the sort of fantasies that must swim inside the heads of all mothers: sleeping past seven in the morning; preparing something other than peanut butter and jelly for lunch; eating slow, leisurely candlelight dinners with my husband (where wine trumps milk as the beverage of choice). This time could nurture so much: my relationship with my spouse as well as the girls' love of their aunt and cousin.

My insides do a little flip when my sister eagerly agrees to a Wednesday pickup. (*Does she realize that potty accidents are a regular occurrence at our house? Or that my eldest refuses to drink any type of juice at breakfast—orange, cranberry, grape?*) I decide to stop worrying and start packing.

"Mama, we are going swimming in Aunt Louise's pool!"

My youngest seems more than a little excited as she stuffs her neon pink goggles and sparkly orange flip-flops in her suitcase.

"We might go to the zoo," says her sister, who I notice is packing her comfort object, a miniature stuffed yellow Big Bird, stained and worn from too much love. *Could she be having reservations about leaving home?*

Before I know it, we are at my sister's home in the country, where her friendly dog and acres of wooded yard welcome our girls.

"Have a good time!" We kiss and hug our children, who already have found new playmates in the neighbor kids next door.

Out the door in a flash, we are free, ready for life without our girls—at least for a few days.

Back home, my husband stretches out on the couch for a nap. I walk around the house, a stranger in my own surroundings. *What should I do?* I look for toys to pick up but find none. Strangely, the laundry baskets are empty. *I guess I could make dinner, but then again, since we are child-free, we should go out to eat. Don't look for work to do, silly. This is your time to relax.*

Listening to my gut, I sit in our sunroom and open a favorite magazine. Just as I begin to read, I hear it, faintly at first, then louder: the neighborhood ice cream truck, calling children with its familiar jingling music. *Oh, how my girls would love a rocket Popsicle.* If they were home, we would be running after the truck right now, waving our hands like fools, then jumping up and down in victory when the truck finally turns down the cul-de-sac, delivering happiness by way of cool frozen confections. But today I simply sit inside.

Dinner, as it turns out, is also disappointing. Water, gushing down Main Street, forces us into our second-choice restaurant, with its second-tier service. (*How can water be pouring from a water main, yet we can't even get a glass of water to drink?*)

"I guess we can't listen to the band," my husband shakes his head, realizing that our evening's entertainment is waterlogged.

Walking down the street, we find an open ice cream shop. *The girls would love the birthday cake flavor or maybe blue cotton candy,* I think. My scoop of butter pecan tastes bittersweet, especially when I eye a family savoring sugar cones on an outside bench.

The next morning, I awaken to eggs, sliced oranges, and freshly brewed coffee, served by my husband, the man who first stole my heart. We enjoy an afternoon of uninterrupted work in our garden, then a romantic outdoor picnic and orchestra concert. Over the next few days, there is time for bookstore browsing, clothes shopping, and dinners of shrimp and chardonnay.

Some day, it will be just us again. The kids will eventually leave home, I muse. This child-free life is pretty great, really. So why do I miss the girls so much?

For me, Wednesday can't come quick enough. It is the Fourth of July, but, truth be told, I think independence is a bit overrated.

"I missed you bunches!" I gush, flying out of the car to hug my girls.

"Mama! Mama! We went to the zoo and rode a camel!"

"We went down a slide at the pool!"

"Let's go to our pool tomorrow," I suggest. "And maybe the ice cream truck will come down our street."

Throwing the kids' suitcases into the trunk, we head home. Giggles and nursery rhymes fill the air, and finally, I am complete.

—Stefanie Wass

Diving In

People say I take after my mother. When I came along, Mom was just age seventeen, in ways a child herself. Still, naïveté didn't stop her from loving her first-born daughter. Above all, my mother was strong.

One day, Mom and I sit on the sofa and thumb through photo albums, reminiscing. I point out our similarities in one of my baby pictures, the one where I'm standing on a wicker chair, holding my Peter Pan doll.

She tells me, "You were the most beautiful baby—and the crankiest."

I smile.

For a colicky infant I was healthy—until November, 1952, when I was eight months old. At that time, Mom, Daddy, and I lived in a small apartment in Phoenix, Arizona. I'd already mastered standing and was on the verge of walking. Mom normally had to run to keep up with me.

"You were always going," she says, "a mile a minute."

But when Mom came to my crib one morning that November, I lay still, looking up at her. Curtains fluttered at the open window. Mourning doves cooed outside. I swear I can remember sunlight streaming through that window, casting the shadows of my crib bars like a ladder along the wall. My usual energy and exuberance had vanished, and I was moving only one of my arms. Instantly, my mother knew something was wrong.

Mom phoned the doctor and her own mother, my Grammie Clark, right away, frantic for answers. "Linda's acting lethargic and she's not moving her left arm," she said.

Perhaps guilt had already ambushed her, knowing I'd fallen out of my high chair the week before. Had I sustained a head injury that was just now causing symptoms? I'm sure she prayed as she and my grandmother rushed me to the doctor's office. At first, the doctor was puzzled too. My head and other faculties tested normal. The high chair fall was ruled out as the cause of my difficulties. Then the doctor made the diagnosis.

Polio. The word struck terror into every parent's core. I'd contracted the often deadly, frequently disabling scourge of the twentieth century. The first vaccines wouldn't arrive for another two years. Knowledge of the day held that people came down with polio, or infantile paralysis, through contact with unsanitary public places. Swimming pools and movie theaters were often closed during epidemics. Families guarded their loved ones, trying to avoid the disease that had crippled President Franklin Delano Roosevelt, put thousands into iron lungs, and claimed the lives of thousands more. In the epidemic of 1952, more than 50,000 polio cases occurred in Phoenix. Mom tells me the county hospital, where most polio victims were sent, was full. Lucky for me, I was admitted to St. Joseph's Hospital, where the level of care was higher.

I was hospitalized for a week, with Mom at my bedside. During my stay, nurses applied wet, hot wool packs to affected areas of my body. Smelly, heavy, and painfully hot, the compresses were meant to stimulate paralyzed muscles into regenerating themselves. They were known as "Sister Kenny treatments," after the Australian nun and nurse who first championed the method, a folk remedy that came to be considered the best treatment available. Mom kept me from wriggling out of the packs and sang lullabies to quiet my crying. The rest of the family tried to comfort my frightened mother while my muscles fought to keep working. For nearly a week, Mom refused to leave my side, even when the hospital's nuns insisted that visiting hours were over.

Doctors said my case was fairly mild, but my left arm and hand would be permanently paralyzed. To a lesser degree, my back and right leg were affected too. Doctors couldn't predict how much I'd recover, only that I'd have to work hard to regain function.

Finally, I was discharged from the hospital. Mom cleaned our apartment, sterilizing everything possible. Now, the real work would begin, along with an avalanche of questions. *Where had Mom taken me that was infected with the virus? What had she done or not done that would have prevented the virus from finding me? Who was to blame?* Like most mothers, mine probably thought it was somehow her fault. Mom must have been disheartened and fearful of the future. In those days, people often kept quiet about misfortune, silently suffering or changing the subject should an ordeal such as mine come up in conversation. Later, science would prove polio is caused by a virus and that over-sterilization contributed to the epidemics.

I gaze at my mother's fading blue eyes, wondering what it must have been like for her. More than fifty years later, she has rarely spoken of my bout with polio.

We turn the photo album's page, and there I am, a three-year-old with my paralyzed arm in an elaborate metal brace that holds my arm up like a shelf.

"What was it like to have a disabled child?" I ask.

Mom glances away and sighs. Even now, talking about my handicap is difficult. But Mom is strong. She tries.

"At first, you scooted around on your bottom," she says.

The progress I'd made toward walking during those first eight months of my life had disappeared.

Mom takes another peek at the photo. "Eventually, though," she says, pointing, "you stood up again and walked, then ran."

Except for my paralyzed arm, I was like any other three-year-old, she assures me.

Mom adds, "You went a mile a minute. I got a workout every day."

She explains that the brace was meant to stabilize my shoulder and keep it from dislocating.

"It sure looks uncomfortable," I say.

She laughs. "You should have seen me trying to get you to wear it."

Between braces and physical therapy, I must have kept her busy. Mom made sure my therapy was intensive. Several days a week, I attended a physical therapy class, and she faithfully helped me do assigned exercises at home. Although she didn't know how to drive a car to get me to the appointments, she plunged into my rehabilitation program.

I turn the album's page once more. A black-and-white snapshot catches my eye. I'm in a bathing suit, perched on the edge of a huge, Olympic-sized swimming pool, about to dive into the water. My pixie-cut hair is wet, plastered to my head. One of my arms dangles, but I'm wearing a big grin.

Mom says, "A Phoenix-area swimmer—an Olympic medalist named Dick Smith—had recovered the use of his legs after he got polio. It was all over the news. I went to his pool, Dick Smith's Swim Gym, and he agreed to help you with water therapy."

Within weeks, she tells me, Smith had me swimming in the deep end of the pool, diving from the high-dive, getting stronger by the day.

I pat the back of her hand. "Grammie told me that you worked for him, doing his bookkeeping or something so I could go there."

She looks away, but nods. "We didn't have much money," she murmurs, "but I wanted you to have the best therapy. I wanted you to be as strong as you could be."

I stare a long moment at the faded photo, willing myself to smell the chlorine, see the aqua water, hear the swim coach's whistle. I can't recollect Dick Smith himself, but I have a sense of my mom there at the Swim Gym, cheering me on. I may have lost the use of one of my arms, but thanks to my mother, I've always dived into life and gone a mile a minute.

We sit side by side on the sofa, two strong women, alike in so many ways.

—Linda Clare

Learning to Fish

I love the way a fly line sounds when it's being cast over the water, like the invisible wings of a thousand mayflies swirling around your body, never touching, but almost. The sound, like the mayfly, will live only a day or two in this fit and start of spring.

It's the first warm day after months of cold, a day that forgot winter isn't over.

The boys were the first to consider the possibility in this unexpected respite from the blustery weather. They woke up this morning, looked out of the grimy window, rubbed their eyes.

Ben said, "I wanna go fishing."

Tyler nodded, like it was the most natural thing in the world to associate blue sky and a spring breeze with a day at the lake. It's been months since they thought about it, but it is that kind of day. A day for shaking off the cocoon of winter. A day for sitting back, letting the sun soak through you and bringing you alive again, like the burst of a daffodil through a still-thawing ground. A great day for fishing.

"Mom, I need that hook now."

I pull my finger out of the tackle box and there are three hooks hanging off it.

"Which kind did you want?"

"Number ten." Ben's pulling in his line. He's got a fly rod.

"Which is that? Big or small?"

"Mom, you really should be more careful."

That's Tyler. He's seven, and I've baited his hook exactly twenty-three times in forty-five minutes.

"It's this one," Ben pulls the smallest out of my finger.

"How come we're not catching anything?" Tyler asks as he holds up his hook.

I stick a salmon egg on it. My fingers are red and sticky from them. I don't think they're real salmon eggs; I think they're synthetic salmon eggs. They kind of look like that fake fruit in Christmas fruitcake.

"I dunno, Ty. Maybe the fish are onto us."

Actually, I've been praying the whole time the boys won't catch anything, because I don't know what to do if they do. I mean, I did look it up on the Internet, so I have an idea, but that isn't the same as actually doing it. It's like the moment you see the little plus sign on the pregnancy test. You know what has to happen; you're just not sure how you're gonna get there, but you know you will. Being a mother is like that.

I've left a red path of fingerprints on my jeans, and now there's lint sticking to my fingers. I resist the urge to lick them or dip them in the lake. There are crawdads near the shore, and they bite.

So far, we're alone at the lake, except for a menacing-looking herd of Canada geese. They've taken possession of our lake for the winter, and I wonder if they'll give it back. They're underneath the cottonwoods on the other side of the lake now, but I can hear them organizing. Will we be voted off the lake? Or perhaps that's just my imagination, a giddiness bred of sudden exposure to sun after a period of darkness.

The truth is, I don't know if I could hold a fish while it dies. I wouldn't have much of a problem if someone else did it. That would make me merely an accessory. Yeah, I'm one of those people who likes to pretend that meat comes in Styrofoam and Saran Wrap.

One day last summer, I took the boys to a bona fide, stocked trout pond. The kind you pay to get into, pay to rent a rod, then pay by the pound for whatever you catch. (They threw in the bait for free.) If you pay a little extra, they clean the fish for you, too.

This pond had rubber matting all around the banks, so you didn't get muddy, or maybe it was so you wouldn't fall in. The boys loved it. They'd each caught a fish within ten minutes of putting in their line. That's when I realized that going there had been a *big* mistake:

"Mom, we should do this every weekend!"

"Can we get our own poles?"

"I want a SpongeBob pole!"

"Can we go to the fishing store when we get home?"

"Why can't we?"

"Well, then what about tomorrow?"

We were in and out of the pay-by-the-pound pond in an hour. By the time we'd left, I thought I'd regained some ground in discouraging the entire fishing thing. I paid them to clean the trout and made sure the boys watched all of it. I thought it would be a good lesson—a good, unspoken lesson.

We left, all a bit blanched from the experience of watching the fish sliced open, blood and intestines washed down the aluminum sideboard to the drain, and I thought I'd never have to do it again.

The truth is, I don't know what I'm doing. A friend once told me that there isn't a single soul on the planet who *really* knows what they're doing. The trick is to pretend that you do. My boys have taught me more than I could've learned in any mothering manual. The truth is, they are teaching me how to be a mother and much more.

It's after lunch, and the warm weather isn't just a morning's tease. Other people are coming out now, trusting the warmth will last another hour or two. There's a Great Dane, as tall as Tyler, who comes by and thrusts his nose into my lap. My chair nearly tips over, but I throw my legs out and catch myself. I wish he'd stay, but he bounds away toward the cottonwoods on the other side of the lake. He almost knocks over a little girl, who's walking this way with her dad.

"Mom! Don't look!" Tyler says this to me in that warning voice that's louder than a whisper but not a speaking voice. More like a hiss.

"Don't look at what?"

"*Shhh!* Never mind." He pulls his fishing hat lower over his eyes.

I feel a little strange, pretending to ignore the girl and her dad coming toward us. I think that's what my son wants me to do, so I'm sitting here, holding still, looking straight ahead, being quiet.

Just as they're about to pass behind us, Tyler throws out a perfect cast, then very casually turns his head and says, "Hi, Cassie."

He knows her!

"Hi, Tyler."

And she knows him! Hunh.

I don't want to see him grow up. I want him to stay like he is forever, because then he won't leave.

"You wanna live with me when I grow up?" Tyler questions me casually as I untangle his line from a bush near the shore. "You can have your own floor."

Sounds like a sweet deal, but I wonder if he'll remember the offer in, say, twenty years—just enough time for him to wish he'd never made it.

"If it's a tree house and I can have the top floor."

Tyler made me six valentines this year. He says he wants to marry me. Ben wrote me a haiku about a blueberry. He wanted to marry me, too, about three years ago, before he didn't want to anymore.

"We should ask Ben to come, too. We could all have our own floors."

"Do you know what the insurance would be on a place like that?" Ben chimes in. "No, I think we should live on the ground."

"But we could have a pulley for the groceries—an electric pulley."

"What if there was a tornado? I couldn't live in a tree house," Ben insists. "Hey, Mom, where's that wooly booger I had?"

It doesn't occur to him to check his line, where he left it. When I don't answer, though, he figures it's something like that and finds it right away.

Ben learned to tie his own flies from a book. Learned how to fish there, too. The wooly booger looks like . . . well, it looks like a mess of brown thread with lots of split ends tied around a hook, and it's probably bigger than the fish they say are in this lake.

"I think I caught something!" Tyler reels in his line like mad, but there's nothing on it.

He throws out another cast. It's perfect. He's got a good arm.

Did you know they have entire stores filled with thread, and chenille, tinsel, and marabou feathers just for tying flies? The first time I took Ben to The Hungry Bass, his tongue fell out of his mouth. Display after display of feathers, threads, and ribbons in myriad colors. I wanted to buy something just because it all looked so pretty. He spent his entire allowance.

"Need another bait, Mom. They got away again!" Tyler's surprised for the 237th time today.

Ben sits down in my shadow with his fly box, pulls out a piece of fuchsia chenille and the scissors.

He'll be content there for hours. He cuts a small piece of the chenille and waves it in front of his face, dreaming of the bass that will inevitably have a taste for pink with a sliver of silver streamer. (You'd be surprised at what fish will eat.)

I both enjoy and envy Ben and Tyler's youth. They remind me of what's important and often enable me to catch a glimpse of life through a different, fresher pair of eyes.

I'm cutting Tyler's old line out of the bush near the shore. I find the old hook with my thumb, and this time it draws a drop of blood. I automatically stick my thumb in my mouth, bait goop and all. I'd like to tell you it tasted like that synthetic candied fruit they put in Christmas fruitcake, but instead I'm hoping we can stop off at the deli on the way home for some nice roast beef sandwiches with horseradish, wrapped in Saran Wrap.

"Whoa! Mom! Did you see *that?*"

Tyler's proud of his cast but doesn't wait for my answer. "Can we have corn on the cob with our fish?"

He still thinks he's gonna catch me dinner.

And maybe he will.

—*Julie Crea*

True North

I'll always regret that you died so soon and I grew up so late. You were gone before I was able to do things for you that I could have done only a few years later. I could have given you season tickets to Oklahoma football games and pretty dresses in bright colors and a real gold bracelet. I could have taken you to see the pyramids of Egypt and Paris ablaze with lights and London on New Year's Eve as Big Ben chimed midnight. I thought we had forever.

You were gone before I knew the questions I would one day ache to ask. My life was still so much about me that I never realized how much I didn't know about you. What were your dreams when you were young? Did you ever love a man other than Dad? What would you have done differently, given a second chance? Who was the person you most admired? I have thousands of questions now, but only you had the answers.

I matured too slowly. When I raised my hand and took my oath as an attorney, you were gone. When I learned that I could be both vulnerable and strong, you were gone. When I helped to build a marriage that has lasted for decades, you were gone. When I wrote books and learned to bake a chocolate cake that is almost as good as yours and found peace within myself, I longed for you to know, but you were gone.

You were gone before I realized what a remarkable woman you were.

Do you remember the day we wanted to buy two ice cream cones at Demar Drug store for a nickel each? We hunted everywhere, but all we could find was nine cents. We could have bought one cone and shared it, I guess, but I think you didn't want Mr. Demar to guess we didn't have another penny. Somehow, you made that seem funny. We laughed until our sides hurt, and you taught me that sharing a laugh and being with someone you love were the sweetest treats of all.

Do you remember the time you were walking me home from kindergarten and I spotted a bud on the branch of a rose bush, which had crept from beneath a garden wall? I wanted to take it with me, but as I ran to pick it, you said, "Wait. Let's see if it blooms by tomorrow. I'll bet it will be even prettier then." In such small ways you taught me life's lessons, such as the need for patience to give a beautiful thing time to grow and the pleasure of watching it blossom.

Do you remember the day I raced in from first grade, shouting that I could read the words, "I can run"? You listened, knowing that was important, and said, "How wonderful! I can't wait to see what you'll learn this afternoon." Your enthusiasm fed my own, and from that day forward, I loved school, loved to learn.

Do you remember the evening during the Great Depression when a man who was hungry knocked on our door? You fixed him a sandwich. We had hardly enough food for the next day, but you said, "I can't turn away someone who has nothing to eat." You taught me that, no matter what, you must be able to live with yourself.

Do you remember when I told you I loved a man and later when I told you love had ended? You listened, as always, but you never pried, never judged. Your arms just opened wide, and you said, "I love you." I learned that listening with an open heart is one of the greatest gifts anyone can give and that love imposes no conditions.

Do you remember when I called, brokenhearted, to tell you I had lost the baby I'd been carrying and was anticipating with such joy? As quickly as you could get to me, you were there. Far too wise to think platitudes could comfort me, you simply held me as we wept together for all that might have been. I learned that shared pain is easier to bear.

Do you remember when I was about eight and we chose a star as our own? It's not impressive, as stars go. We didn't want to share it and thought that if we picked this little one, tucked close to the Big Dipper, maybe no one else would claim it. Besides, we could always find it there. We wished on it together as you held me tight. "Each time you see our star," you said, "each time for the rest of your life, remember how I love you and that I will always be watching over you."

On this clear winter night, I came outside to look at the stars. I searched the heavens and wondered: *How many billions of stars are out there? Are we alone in the universe? Is there a planet in one of those far-off worlds where someone looks toward our sun and asks the same questions?* I gazed upward at light that traveled thousands of years to touch us in our time and felt part of a universe where time and distance have no meaning, where galaxies whirl forth in harmony with God's great plan. You understand it all now, Mom, but I can only catch a glimmer, like the light of some distant star, glimpsed for a moment, that I cannot find again.

You've been gone for years, and I no longer believe that stars make wishes come true. Yet, I always look for our star and feel comforted. I found it again tonight and smiled, warm in the midst of December. Mom, you taught me that it isn't the great questions of the universe that matter, it's the one simple answer to it all: love.

Do you remember how I used to write poems? They weren't very good, but you always thought they were wonderful. Here's another:

Star Light, Star Bright
A small, steady star lights the heavens
In a place that knows no lies,
Where I'm a child forever,
And memory never dies.
However far I wander,
It never disappears,
And there your love shines, waiting,
True North for all my years.

—*Ramona John*

Sister Rita
Maureen and Mom

Sister Rita Maureen thought I was mentally deficient. That's what she told my parents in her blunt, matter-of-fact way.

"Mr. and Mrs. Brown," she said, peering at them through slanted, pink-framed eyeglasses. "It's the end of the first quarter of school and Cathy can't read. Something's very wrong with her." She looked away, embarrassed. "I think you know what I mean."

There was stunned silence in the first-grade classroom. And then my mother was suddenly overwhelmed with tears. Dad snapped to attention. Nobody, not even a nun, was permitted to make my mother cry. And no one, not even a nun, should dare to suggest that one of his children was even remotely less than perfect.

"Sister Rita Maureen," he said. "I think there's something very wrong with the teacher."

It still shocks me to the end of my toes that Dad would talk to a sister like that. Dad was as good a Catholic as they come. But he was very angry.

I didn't hear about this story until years later. But looking back, it explains a lot. Sister Rita Maureen never did warm up to me. How could she? Vatican II was barely out of the gates and Dad had done the unthinkable: he had been disrespectful to a nun. According to pre-Vatican II tradition, he and all his offspring would burn in hell.

I don't know why I couldn't read. That first day of first grade, I walked the half block to school with lofty ambitions and fully expected to come home reading vast volumes. But I had attended a different kindergarten across town. All the other first graders at my new Catholic school seemed to have a jump on me.

After the first week, Sister sent me with a copy of *Dick and Jane* to sit by the radiator with Group 3. The Loser Group. We all knew it. We were the handful of stupid kids who were relegated to the back of the room so that Sister Rita Maureen could get on with the real business of teaching. I'd leaf through *Dick and Jane* and stare at the big vibrant pictures. Jane and her little sister Sally fascinated me. They wore different color-coordinated outfits every day. Dresses, hair ribbons, socks—they all matched. I longed to know them. They looked like such happy girls.

After that fateful parent-teacher conference, Sister Rita Maureen ignored me completely. But it didn't matter. Mom had decided to take matters into her own hands. One afternoon, I came home after school to see flash cards lined up across the back of the couch in the TV room.

"Today," Mom announced, "you're learning to read."

We started with consonants. Then she taught me the sounds of all the vowels. I remember the first word I ever read: cat. So much like my own name! I stared in wonder at Mom.

She smiled her beautiful smile and said, "See? That's all there is to it."

After that, I sounded out every single word I could find—on street signs, cereal boxes, and toothpaste tubes. Then one magical day, Mom walked me over to the library at Montview and Clermont, and I walked out with five books and a library card of my own. Nothing before or since has ever given me such satisfaction. Learning to read simply changed my whole world.

In Sister Rita Maureen's classroom, I was still sitting by the radiator. But by now, I had become intimately acquainted with Dick, Jane, Sally, Spot, Puff, and the whole cast of characters. On my own, I read the stories of their lives. I was too absorbed to be unhappy.

One day, however, Sister called Group 3 to the front. This was a surprise. Our little group roused itself and trooped to the front of the room.

"Open your books," Sister Rita Maureen ordered us. "Read, Cathy." She fixed me with her steely pale blue eyes.

So I read. Sister forgot to tell me to stop. I read three pages before I finally took a breath and looked up. Every kid in the room was staring at me in astonishment. It hit me in that instant—I was the best reader in the class. I smiled up at Sister Rita Maureen. She was astounded.

Suddenly, she snapped her mouth shut. "Well," she cleared her throat. "Aren't you something," she said primly. That was all.

I have been a teacher for more than thirty years now. But it was a long time before I really understood why I even wanted to teach. It was because of first grade. In the first grade, I learned the greatest lesson of my life. For that, I'm grateful to Sister Rita Maureen. She taught me that a teacher's smallest touch, word, or look can be so powerful that it can change the entire way a child thinks about herself. My mom taught me the very same thing.

—*Cathy Howard*

An Ordinary Day

It is 10:15 A.M. on a hot August morning. I've been up with my three children for nearly four hours and accomplished one thing: everyone has been fed. Kevin, my two-month-old infant, has been nursed and settled in for his short morning nap. I've poured Cheerios and milk into a bowl and peeled a banana for my three-year-old daughter, Kristin. She's now feeding her Cabbage Patch Kid doll, Miles, his breakfast in the family room. Somehow, I've also managed to encourage, cajole, and finally force Brian, age five, to swallow most of a bowl of soggy Kix soaked in Ensure. I've wiped down the kitchen table, Brian's high chair, the floor, and the countertops. This process will all begin again in just over an hour when it's time for lunch.

I pause at the kitchen sink and drink the lukewarm glass of orange juice I poured for myself an hour ago. While staring out the kitchen window at nothing, I hear Mr. Rogers in the background. In his nearly hypnotic voice, he announces that today we are going to learn about zippers. Yesterday, we learned about crayons, the day before that it was graham crackers, and today it's zippers. The telephone rings, abruptly jarring me out of my temporary blankness.

My son Brian was diagnosed at the age of two with a rare, terminal genetic disease called Niemann Pick disease, Type C (NPC). We were told he would not live beyond the age of fifteen. Overnight, I became the mother of a child with special needs, a job I've now held for three years.

I have been waiting three days for a return phone call from the head of a new special education preschool program recommended to me for Brian by our social worker. Maybe, just maybe, the ringing phone is her, finally getting back to me. "Hello?" I say anxiously.

I'm immediately relieved to learn it's the head of the special-education preschool program. She introduces herself, including all the capital-lettered degrees after her name, and then, without taking a breath, she launches into all the wonderful and amazing merits, benefits, and positive attributes of this special program for special children and their special families. Ten minutes into her sales pitch, I've barely mumbled more than two "uh-huhs."

She finishes with this declaration: "And we're certain that this special program is perfect for Brian. With our ratio of one teacher and one aide to every five children with special needs, we can teach Brian the skills necessary for him to take care of his own needs—work with him on his potty training, to put on his own socks, button his own shirt, even zip his own jacket."

I look over at Brian, propped in the corner of the sofa, where I put him after taking him out of his high chair. He's able to sit there in an upright position only with the support of six strategically placed pillows and his Puffalump. His head is slumped over, and drool from his breakfast is oozing out from the side of his mouth onto his clean shirt. I forgot to put a fresh bib on him again. He's making a gurgling sound and reaching out with his bent hand, trying to get Kristin's attention. She's become mesmerized by Mr. Rogers's calm voice and is focused on learning about zippers.

As the program director drones on, I watch Kristin feed her doll a bowl of pretend cereal, a make-believe banana, and a bottle. Next, I know she will clean up after Miles and then get him dressed, because, at age three, she imitates nearly everything

I do. She is potty trained, can feed herself, and manages to dress herself with little help. She has learned to do what "normal" toddlers do.

I think of my newborn, Kevin, sleeping soundly in his crib in his nursery down the hall. He eats well, nearly sleeps through the night, and is beginning to smile. He is doing what eight-week-old babies do. In the medical jargon my husband and I are so familiar with now, Kristin and Kevin are referred to as the "unaffected" siblings.

Of course, it's a given that our "normal" children will develop and evolve from a state of total dependence to one of independence. As parents, it is our job to guide them and teach them to become self-sufficient. We can confidently expect and depend upon the fact that their need for us as their physical caretakers will diminish year by year. As the mother of two normal, healthy children, I know that if I do my job right, I will eventually work myself out of a job. In return, I can anticipate being rewarded with the privilege of watching them grow into strong, competent adults. That is not the case in my job as the mother of a child with special needs.

It is impossible not to make comparisons between Brian's development and that of his younger sister and baby brother. Although he developed normally for about a year, since then he has regressed in every possible way. He can no longer sit unsupported, feed himself, or walk. He is completely wheelchair-bound. He communicates only with undecipherable grunts and groans and irregular, jerky gestures. He has seizures, despite the medication he's on to prevent them. Aside from his physical care, I maintain his "administrative" and medical care along with a team of specialists: doctors, neurologists, physical therapists, social workers, teachers, teacher aides, and the driver of Brian's short yellow school bus. It is a daunting, daily challenge.

Even bedtime brings little relief, to Brian or to me. He wakes up several times a night requiring a repositioning or help to clear his respiratory congestion. More often than not, I sit blindly in the dark on the edge of his bed, rubbing his head and his back, trying to guess what the problem could be, trying to figure out what to do for him. I often feel helpless. I cannot stop Brian's crying; I cannot take away his pain; I cannot make it better. I cannot do what a good mother is supposed to do: comfort and protect her child. This thought nearly suffocates me.

Eventually, Brian's cries do subside. He finally falls asleep. I leave his room with the fleeting feeling that I have helped to ease his pain, if only for the next few hours. It is a hollow hope, though, because I know that sleep came because he was overcome by exhaustion and that this quiet time and his peaceful sleep are only temporary.

In those hours, when I slump against the wall in the hallway and try to catch my breath, I face the stark reality that I never will be able to protect my child from this pain and that the comfort I provide will never be enough to completely relieve it.

As the woman on the phone drones on, I look over at Brian again. For the moment, he has a half smile on his face. *Is he happy? Or, this time, is his smile merely reflexive?* I'm never quite sure. Most often, it's an involuntary expression. I wish he could tell me. I wish he could be happy, if even for a moment.

Finally, the woman pauses to take a breath, and I grab the chance to ask if she has talked to Brian's teacher or aide.

"No, I've been out of town at a conference until today," she answers.

I ask if she has talked to Brian's social worker.

"No, like I said, I've been out of town at a conference in Chicago. However, she is on my list to call next."

I ask if she has Brian's files in front of her.

"Well, no, but I'm assuming—"

I cut her off and lead into my memorized, pre-programmed description of Brian, his disease, and the state of his condition at this point. Then, I stop and wonder, *What is the point? Let her assume away,* I think.

I say: "You know, this special program sounds perfect. Sign Brian up. If you can teach him to put on his own socks, button his own shirt, or zip his own jacket, you are one amazing genius!" Well, "amazing" is not exactly the adjective I used. And I do not add that Brian is still in diapers.

I hear dead air. *Is she still there?*

There are days like this when I simply run out of patience and self-restraint. Days when I am not pleasant or polite to those "experts" who, for the most part, have Brian's best interests in mind. And there are days when I am flat-out mean, nasty, and ungrateful to those people. Lately, those days seem to have become the norm.

There are also days when I desperately want to forget that I've ever heard the word "special"—special needs, special children, special families. On those days, I crave ordinary. Today, especially, I crave ordinary.

I politely say thank you and end the call.

I walk down the hallway and look in on Kevin, see that he is still sound asleep. I reach out to touch his soft skin, his silky hair, but stop short, not wanting to wake him up.

I return to the family room, where Kristin is busy with her make-believe chores. I lean over and give her a kiss on the top of her sweet-smelling head. Then I go and sit next to Brian on the couch. I hold up his head and cradle it gently in my arms so he can see the television.

Kristin is now rocking Miles to sleep on her lap. The three of us are lulled into a cocoon of normalcy by the unflappable, reassuring voice of Mr. Rogers. I ask Kristin if she could turn up the TV a little bit so Brian can learn about zippers, too.

—Linda Avery

Growing Wise

A marvelous thing has happened. After years of being a mom who didn't know anything, I've suddenly become the Wise One. But the transformation wasn't mine; it was my son's. When Michael and his wife had a baby, I gained exalted status in his mind.

"How did you ever manage with four kids?" he asked. "You must have been a saint."

As a mom whose child-raising concepts were often ignored or met with indifference, I was surprised by my son's revelation.

During his college years—when Michael knew all there was to know about Life, Kids, and Good Times—he often tried to advise me on raising his little sister, who was eight years younger than he. From his vantage point, I had it all wrong—no matter that I'd already feathered three birds (including him) and sent them out of the nest, safely and successfully.

"You should spend more time with her," he admonished when she was in middle school and he was off to college (and not really aware of what was going on at home).

Of course, he forgot that I had gone back to work full-time and didn't have the luxury of daytime catering that I'd had when he was his younger sister's age.

According to Michael, we didn't supervise her enough. "You let Suzanne go out too much," he warned when she was in high school. With fresh memories based on his own experiences, he wanted his sister confined more than he had been. That was the way he saw it (from a distance). But remembering his own high school experiences, Michael also wanted his sister—a girl, after all!—confined even more than he had been. She had too many privileges, he said. We didn't make her do what he remembered having to do himself—in a selective memory that usually forgot the details of his own escapades. When he was a teenager, I cringed when I answered the phone and heard, "Hey, Mom, guess what?" from the other end. That greeting was usually followed by the admission that he had either (a) just brown-nosed his professor out of a bad grade, (b) received a speeding ticket, or (c) was at the police station—and not to hand out donuts.

This money-minded fellow (later a Harvard Business School graduate) has never shied from giving advice. During the high-tech boom of the late 1990s, he talked me into buying a dotcom stock he knew was destined for greatness. As predicted, in a matter of months it doubled in value, so I held on. When the bubble burst, the price fell quickly, and I eventually sold what remained for pennies on the dollar.

"You still have that stock?" Michael asked incredulously, when I chided him about his can't-miss tip. "I sold out long ago," he said.

Michael gave me advice to buy; he forgot to mention when to sell.

Still, Michael is sensitive and caring in his own way. He noticed difficulties I was having during the split with his father and supported my decisions wholeheartedly. After I had later remarried, he observed, "You used to cry all the time. Now you don't cry anymore." On Father's Day he sent my new husband a card with the personal note: "Thanks for taking good care of my mom."

Then his own baby was born—the first birth in the world that mattered—and the miracle of understanding hit him like a lightning bolt. Every night for the first week of his baby's life, Michael called me long distance and talked for hours. Not about his precious baby but about the fact that he was now a DAD. And about the mysteries of life. And about the responsibilities of parenthood. And about his fears and anxieties for this tiny creature entrusted to his care. And about how utterly exhausted he was.

"I can't believe how much time a baby takes," he sighed.

He continued to nervously chat about "the state of the world" for another half hour. I listened patiently as he stumbled around, trying to fit himself into this new role.

"Just love your baby and the details will work out," I told him. "You'll get to rest soon enough."

And it turned out that his son was an excellent sleeper, didn't break or melt when bathed, and the sun rose each day despite all those worries.

After a year or so, Michael claimed to have this parenting thing figured out. He was convinced that Perfect Parents raise Perfect Kids. Forget all that stuff regarding genetics and the inborn nature of each human being. Nurture took center stage in his home. All it takes to make easy-to-care-for kids is loving parents, he declared. Can't understand why your child has colic, won't sleep all night long, and fusses when he's wet or hungry? Look in the mirror.

Trouble is, his newly acquired knowledge didn't hold up when the second child was born with a less compliant nature than the first. After raising four children, all with different personalities and temperaments, I know, as do other parents, that children cannot be classified so simply. Too many factors are out of our control. From the instant of conception, each baby is unique, as different from any other human as his fingerprint. And I'll share these insights with Michael . . . if and when he asks.

When my son praises me for values instilled in him at a young age—work hard, save your money, be kind—I remind him that most of who he is was determined before he came into the world. He was born excited and excitable, and that hasn't changed. Being a cash-conscious kid, at four years of age he could count out any combination of coins to equal a dollar. At age ten, he started mowing yards and saved his earnings to buy a car when he reached the legal driving age of sixteen. He mercilessly teased the two sisters who bookended him in age and lovingly cared for his baby sister. None of that was taught. He just did it because that's who he is—a loving guy with an innate drive to succeed and a middle child's need to nurture.

With the birth of his first child, I became Super Mom, the one with all the answers. The one to discuss evolution with. The one he credits with allowing him to have a great job, beautiful wife, and comfortable home before he turned thirty. Well, thanks for the accolades, dear, and I love having long phone conversations with you, but I just did what I had to do in the best way I could. I learned parenting on the job, and my advice reflects that learning process. Nature often overruled nurture, and that was a good thing. Feeling appreciated, even revered, is blissful, although I believe parents really can't take credit for all of their children's successes any more than they should take unwarranted blame for their children's failures. But Michael won't learn that for another twenty years.

Raising kids is like throwing darts. You may be lucky and hit the bull's-eye, or your dart could just as easily miss the target. Either way, it's best to just enjoy the game. For now, I'll savor the wonder of my wisdom. I'll revel in Michael's praise, however fleeting. The day will come when my advice won't be needed or wanted. Still, I'm glad he asked. Someday, when he becomes Exalted Dad, maybe he'll remember that I was wise once—and passed along that wisdom to him.

—*Beverly Burmeier*

Look Out,
Wonder Woman!

lready that morning, I'd cleaned up the remnants of a broken cereal bowl, nursed a knee boo-boo back to orthopedic health, and chased after our belligerent dog, who'd taken one look at my pleading eyes when I called him in—*You talkin' to me?*—and bolted out of the yard.

When the preteen bickering started up, I knew I needed all the strength I could muster, and I drew it from my mother's words, spoken just the week before.

"Don't you know, my dear, you're Wonder Woman?" she'd said.

I was still on a maternal high from her compliment: nothing was too much for me now, not even today's episode of raging hormones.

"He called me stupid!"

"She tried to trip me!"

"I just went like this."

A replay of the alleged tripping followed: one foot took a slightly exaggerated step, obviously kept in check for the sake of argument—which promptly started up again.

"It's a free country; I can walk funny if I want to."

I could feel myself spinning, making that magical transformation from Mom to Wonder Woman, from bed head and pajamas—spin—to bouffant hair and gaudy gymnastics outfit, complete with gold stars and red, knee-high boots. The kids didn't seem to notice.

"You can't walk funny if you're going to trip me!"

"I did not trip you!"

"Enough!" I said. "You go to your room. And you go to yours." I didn't have to use names, just the magic of pointing. (Where was my golden lasso when I needed it?)

First came one slamming door, then the other. I hesitated on the stairs. I exhaled, closed my eyes for a few seconds, felt for the golden band around my head—still intact—and went on to the kitchen, where I found my three little ones waiting patiently at the table for their breakfast.

While muffled complaints wafted down the stairs, I mindlessly poured juice and sprinkled cinnamon on toast. This was definitely a superhero skill: I could do these simple tasks while I mapped out the evening's driving routes in my head, figured out who would get where and when, who would have to go a little early or wait a little late. I could even call out reminders—"I said stay in your rooms!"—while my brain calculated how long it would take to get from one end of the city (soccer) to another (dance studio).

Each day had become a Rubic's cube, waiting to be solved—and solve it I did. No puzzle was too daunting for Wonder Woman. Today, however, posed a particular challenge. On top of the usual dance, piano lessons, soccer practice, and swim team, we had a school orchestra concert. How would I get to the concert on time? It figured that on a night with an extra activity I'd be on my own. My husband would be working late; I couldn't rely on him for the Super Parent tag-team routine.

"I'll be coming straight to the concert from swimming tonight," I said to my daughter as she and her brother left for school, one contrite, the other still sulking.

She gave me a reluctant cheek to kiss; her repentant brother planted one right on my lips.

"It ends fifteen minutes before . . ." I let my voice trail.

She wasn't listening. Didn't she know the feat I would perform just to be there tonight?

"I'll be at your concert," I said, imagining the grand entrance we'd make into the school auditorium: a woman in body suit and go-go boots, a toddler on her hip, and trailing behind, one wet-haired swimmer, one muddy soccer player, and one ballerina. My daughter hated making a scene. How would she like this one?

"Just don't be late," she warned and shut the door.

After school, the kids piled in my oversized SUV, and Superhero Mom began the circuitous journey about town. The two younger ones were used to this and loved it; they'd done it since they were born. The older kids were in and out by turns. Last stop before the concert: swim practice. I breathed a sigh of relief when we pulled up in front of the pool and swimmer boy was already standing there, disheveled wet hair, towel and goggles dangling from his gym bag. The girls had nothing on this guy: he could shower for thirty minutes after practice and say he'd barely gotten wet. This time, he'd hurried. Yes!

We had to park a few blocks away from the school auditorium. Carrying one child and holding hands with two—another superhero trick—I made my way to the school, found a seat near the back, and listened with four of my lovely brood to a typical middle school orchestra concert. Upon the last note—and I mean right when the conductor dropped his hands—I jumped up from my seat and gathered the kids to leave.

Success! I thought. I'd pulled it off, and now I was thinking of the dinner that sat in the Crock-Pot at home, waiting for us. It would be late, but we'd eat something healthy and we'd eat together. I was good at that, too. I watched other families pick up fast food on days like this, just to fill their children's bellies. Not Wonder Woman. I made nutritious meals every day—rain, shine, or hectic schedule.

My daughter joined us, and we wound our way over to the car. I could hear her viola case hitting her leg with the rhythm of each step, her performance shoes click-clacking along the sidewalk. I was still patting myself on the back, thinking that my blue and red body suit was surely visible to the world, when suddenly my daughter came to a quick and purposeful halt. Her little brother stopped short just before running into her.

"You're so rude!" she yelled, looking straight at me.

If people hadn't noticed me for my superhero suit, they'd certainly noticed me now, not for the garish outfit but for the tall, gangly girl in white and black confronting her mother.

"What?" I said, cocking my head and furrowing of my brow.

"Did you even like the concert?" she asked. Her face was stone.

"Of course," I said. "It was great."

"Then why didn't you say anything? You didn't even tell me 'Good job' or 'That was great.'" I thought

I saw a tear before she turned away and resumed her step.

"That was great!" the kids all said in unison.

I knew it should have come from me. There was no do-over, nothing to get those moments back to tell her how much I enjoyed listening to her play. No way to go back in time, pull myself together, drop the drama, and be a mom, pure and simple. All this time, I was trying to be a superhero when what I needed to be was a mother. What good was it to be Wonder Woman if I didn't take time to pat my child on the back, encourage her, tell her she's wonderful? Preteens have a way of telling it exactly how they see it. They're not always right, of course, but when they are, look out! That evening, my daughter was right. And after we discussed other, better ways of dealing with frustration and disappointment, we talked about other, better ways of handling busy schedules, never losing sight of how important family is.

I'm still Wonder Woman—what mother isn't? But I don't need the body suit or red boots to prove it. My kids don't even care for that. What they need is someone who slows down long enough to offer kind words and a caring touch—the love of a mother.

—*Glenys Loewen-Thomas*

Here Beside Me

Brennan cried out from his crib, and I hurried to get him before he woke Liddy. He dropped his head on my shoulder and threaded his fingers through my curls. He was still a baby himself, not even two, but I seldom held him like that anymore, with three-month-old Liddy so often needing me.

Liddy was born with complications—swollen kidneys, an elevated white blood cell count because she and I had conflicting blood types, a heart murmur caused by a congenital heart defect, and a dimple in her spine that could signal more serious problems. Most of these issues simply required monitoring to ensure they resolved themselves. But Liddy also had severe reflux, a digestive disorder that kept her chronically underweight and vulnerable to breathing problems. I rarely left her, and then only with my husband John or with my mother, when she came in town to help. We had just moved to a new neighborhood and had no family close by, but my mother came often. She understood Liddy's and Brennan's needs—and mine.

With Brennan still on my shoulder, I heard Liddy chirp from my bedroom. I peered down the hallway to where my mother sat in the living room.

"Mom, can you get Liddy?"

I saw her hop up from her chair as I stepped back into Brennan's room to hold him a minute longer.

Suddenly, a heavy thud shook the floor. Brennan jerked upright in my arms.

"Hey," I smiled, wanting to reassure him. "What the heck was that?"

I carried him to my bedroom and found Liddy alone, asleep in her bassinet. I walked through the empty kitchen, the dining room, the living room. Confused, I turned in a circle. My mother had disappeared. I walked back into my bedroom. My mother was on the floor, and still. Lying with her back to me, she wore blue jeans and her favorite denim shirt— the one she left hanging in my closet between visits, a small thing that marked her intention to return soon. I could see the white-blonde bob of her hair, but her face was somehow hidden by the comforter draping from my bed.

"Mom?"

She didn't move. I set Brennan down.

"Mom?"

Silence. Stillness.

In a sudden rush of adrenaline, I moved to get the phone and dialed 9-1-1, ran back to the bedroom, dropped to the floor, and pressed my hand to Mom's shoulder.

"My mother has fallen unconscious," I told the 9-1-1 dispatcher. Those were the words that came to mind, strangely precise: my mother had fallen, unconscious.

But a few seconds later, my mother opened her eyes and I wanted to cry out in relief.

"Mom, you passed out," I said, then told the dispatcher that she was conscious again.

My mother sat up, startlingly alert. She shook her head. "I didn't pass out."

"You did," I said. "I heard you fall."

The dispatcher asked questions: "Is she breathing and speaking normally? Is she disoriented?"

"All fall?" Brennan asked, his language plucked from endless rounds of ring-around-the-rosy."

"Yes, Grandma Mary fell. But she's okay."

"Karen," my mother said, her tone reducing me to the role of recalcitrant teenager. "I did not pass out."

I spoke into the phone. "She seems fine now. But she was unconscious. I heard her fall."

I looked apologetically at my mother, who sat looking back at me as though I had lost my mind, leading me to wonder if I had, if perhaps she had simply lain down for a rest and I had misinterpreted, over-reacted in the most dramatic possible way. The dispatcher said she would send an ambulance anyway.

"I just can't believe I passed out," my mother said. She told me she'd gone to my bedroom and seen Liddy settling back into sleep, so she'd sat down on my ottoman for a minute to watch her.

"You're on the floor," I said.

She couldn't argue with that. She sighed and, despite my protests, slowly got to her feet. Brennan and I followed her into the dining room. I gave her a glass of water, which she calmly set down on the end table and ignored. I called John, who said he would take the train right home.

"That better not be sirens," my mother said when we heard the approaching ambulance.

I sat Brennan in front of the TV and stuck in a Barney video. I opened the door and watched the EMTs get out of the truck. They moved slowly, and one went back into the ambulance for something he seemed to have forgotten; the word "bumbling" came to mind.

"You're going to love these guys," I laughed to my mother to ease the tension.

But they came in with an air of competence and I felt relief. It had been right to call. They would check her out and tell us she was fine. Jay was slight, handsome, and he spoke in a warm voice. Doug was heavyset and efficient and seemed to be in charge. They worked in concert, Doug setting up equipment on the kitchen table while Jay asked my mother questions. They stayed within arm's reach of her.

Then, suddenly, she was turning gray, fading again. She murmured that she felt sick, just as Liddy began crying from the bedroom.

I ran to get the baby and hurried back to see Jay and Doug lowering my semiconscious mother to the kitchen floor. Jay pulled open her shirt and cut through her tank top to place monitors on her naked chest.

After placing Liddy in her infant seat on the floor, I grabbed a list of phone numbers off the refrigerator. Most were friends from our old neighborhood. I dialed Lucy, the one new neighbor who had visited our house. I tried to filter out Liddy's cries, the grating voices on the television, and the harsh static of the radio, and instead focus on the EMTs words and Lucy's voice on the phone, which turned out to be her answering machine.

Liddy's cries became screams, and I looked up to see that her seat had tipped over and spilled her onto the floor. I picked her up and held her to me. "I'm here," I said. "I'm so sorry."

I looked at the EMTs tending to my mother, understanding that they would need to take her, certain only that I needed to go, too. John wasn't there, and the one other person I could trust with Liddy— the person I'd come to rely on more now than when I was a child myself, it seemed—was being lifted onto a stretcher.

I asked Doug if I could leave Liddy behind while I ran to get a neighbor. Then I pulled Brennan's puffy yellow jacket around him and told him we were going to run to Lucy's house to see if she was home. No one answered the door. I frantically scanned the houses up and down the street. The sage-colored house on the corner was lit warmly from within. John had mentioned them: a nice couple with two kids. I pulled Brennan close and ran up their steps. A woman opened the door and looked past me to see the flashing lights of the ambulance and the fire rescue truck pulling in behind it. The woman, Jill, reached for Brennan before I said a word.

"I have a baby, too, at the house," I said. "Can you come with us?"

When we reached the front steps, my upstairs neighbor, Alison, was waiting at my door. Inside, my mother still lay on the kitchen floor. Jill took

Brennan from my arms, and Alison lifted a crying Liddy from her infant seat.

Several large men crowded the small space between my mother and me. "I'm right here, Mom," I called.

She turned her head to look at me. She appeared completely at ease. "Where is Brennan?" she asked.

I told her he was fine, that he was watching *Barney*.

The men arranged my mother on the stretcher. They examined the narrow doorways and wondered whether they could make the turns. They opened a closet door for extra room. Finally, they lifted her. And I was grabbing my wallet, my keys, my mother's small suede purse, and calling out goodbyes to Brennan and Liddy—Liddy, who never left my sight. And promising, praying, that John would be home soon.

Outside, in the quiet red glare of the ambulance lights, where my mother had already, again, disappeared, I stopped and caught a sob in my throat. Then Doug reached an arm out to me and guided me up into the high passenger's seat of the ambulance and, in as kind a gesture as I've known, reached over me to pull the seatbelt across my lap and buckle me in.

At the hospital, I climbed out of the ambulance into the dark evening to see my mother being whisked through the emergency room's double doors on the stretcher. I followed inside, where the over-bright ER was filled with people, noise, and activity. I talked with an attendant and provided basic information about my mother: name, address, date of birth. When he asked about her insurance, I looked into her small suede purse and the sight of her few, neatly ordered things made me ache for her. Afterward, I stood and leaned against a wall in the packed waiting room, alone among strangers, waiting.

A short while later, my mother opened her eyes when I walked into the tiny curtained examination room, but she barely moved. She whispered that she was nauseous. But after a nurse gave her a pill, she gradually began to seem herself again.

"Everyone likes my socks," she smiled, wiggling her toes in the socks decorated with black cats that I had given her.

A cardiologist came in and said my mother was stable but that they would need to admit her to run some tests. After getting settled into a room and calling her husband, my mother told me to go home to my kids.

I called a taxi and walked outside into the crisp night air. I caught my breath, held it, and then gave in to tears. I dialed my sister.

"Everything's fine," I told her. "Everything's okay. I just can't stop crying."

For three days the doctors tested and monitored my mother. I drove to the hospital between Liddy's feedings, and John visited, too, bringing her magazines and fresh bread, olives, and cheese. He found her eyeglasses on my bedroom floor. But we never learned for certain what had caused the fainting episodes. The doctors speculated about a virus, dehydration, and a newly diagnosed heart murmur, a tiny hole in her heart, just like Liddy's.

"I can't be alone with my grandchildren until I know why this happened," my mother said when she came home to us. She looked at Liddy. "I won't hold her."

"Maybe when you're sitting down," I said.

But I knew right away that I had said the wrong thing. For all of our sakes, I needed to replace the scary images in my head with the reality I was so fortunate to be living—a mother who was healthy and strong and here beside me as I learned to be a mother, too.

"Take her," I said, holding Liddy out.

My mother moved toward a chair but I stopped her.

"Just take her," I said.

She hesitated. Then she took Liddy into her arms. She touched her cheek to Liddy's forehead, and I turned and left them there.

—Karen Dempsey

Dear God,
Don't Let Me Laugh!

I'm in the cleaning supplies aisle at the supermarket, pulling with all my might on a plunger stuck to the floor. Shoppers stare as they squeeze around me. I want to apologize. Really I do. But I don't dare, because if I did, I'd have to look up from the floor and let all those mature, responsible adults see that I'm quietly laughing my head off.

If anyone else were struggling to remove a plunger that her nine-year-old had stuck to the floor, I'd have every right to laugh. But, of course, you don't do that when you're the mom. The mom is supposed to take these matters seriously. She's supposed to give her child The Look. She's supposed to scold him in The Tone. The last thing in the world she's supposed to do is laugh. That just might make her child think a shopping trip wouldn't be complete without a plunger stuck to the floor.

But do I really have to stifle myself until Kevin goes off to college? Aren't there any other mothers out there who can't stifle their amusement when their kids do or say something inappropriate but also downright funny?

Goodness knows, my mother didn't have this problem. I swear she was born with the demeanor of Mother Superior. She takes pride in telling people about the time, when I was about three, that I looked up at her after doing something naughty and said, "Mommy, make a pretty face."

I suspect most women, though, lose their sense of humor along the way to motherhood, probably around the twenty-third hour of labor. Take my friend Lori, for instance. Lori managed to raise two responsible teenagers who wouldn't have dreamed of sticking a plunger to a supermarket floor. But when the two of us were in college together, Lori had no more control over the giggles than I did. Case in point: one day in microbiology class, the professor walked in from outside with two windblown tufts of hair sticking up like a devil's horns. Lori and I were in stitches. Just as one of us started to calm down, we'd look at the other and start tittering all over again. For some reason I still don't understand, nobody else in the class laughed. I guess they were honing their parenting skills.

Of all the times Kevin makes me laugh, the most embarrassing are when he has no intention of being funny. Like when he sings. Ever since a nun made me lip synch to avoid throwing everyone else off at the Christmas concert in fifth grade, I've been too self-conscious to sing anywhere but in the car with the windows shut. I didn't want my son to grow up like that. So from the time he was born, I started singing to him in the car with the windows shut. Then one day, we were driving along and a song he knew came on the radio, and he started singing. I've never heard anyone so flat, so incapable of carrying a tune, so much like me. I tried to control myself, but it was more than I could bear. I burst out laughing. I wracked my brain for an excuse. Thank goodness, it hit me in a flash; I told Kevin I was laughing about something our neighbor Bill had said the day before. I went on to explain that Bill had pointed out— truthfully, I might add—that every third word out of our neighbor Roger's mouth is "subsequently." Kevin never questioned my laughing at something I'd heard twenty-four hours earlier. He knew me too well.

Another time that Kevin gave me a fit of giggles without trying was when he called his friend Christian and Christian's mother picked up the phone.

"Hi, Sheila," he said. "This is Kevin."

Sheila? To an adult from a fourth-grader? That's like me calling the queen of England "Liz." I started giggling, which made Kevin laugh. Now, Sheila not only thinks my son is all too casual addressing adults but downright rude, too.

Church, of course, is one of those places where every parent must show by example that it's never appropriate to laugh. I wish to God I knew how. My husband Bob, Kevin, and I were in church one Sunday, listening to a priest with a heavy foreign accent. The priest wanted to teach us the importance of "keeping our word," which he pronounced "keeping our wood." *Nothing funny about that*, I told myself. *I'm in church. I am not going to laugh.* Then the priest told us again to "keep our wood." I squeezed my lips together and stared at my lap. The third "wood" was the killer. My shoulders started shaking. Tears rolled down my cheeks. I fought to keep from laughing out loud. My husband and everyone else around me were stoic, as you'd expect of people listening to a sermon about holding onto lumber. Everyone, of course, except me and my son.

Life has changed a lot since those days. Now that Kevin's sixteen, I see him in spurts, usually when I'm driving him from school to Kyle's house, or from Kyle's house to Taylor's house, or from Taylor's house to Max's house, or from Taylor's house to ours. The few waking hours Kevin spends at home are in his room, usually texting Kyle, Taylor, Max, and every other teenager within a twenty-five-mile radius. I'm grateful, though, that one precious thing hasn't changed: his sense of humor.

I was reminded of that recently, when I took Kevin to an empty parking lot to teach him how to drive a stick shift. He jerked forward, then stopped, jerked forward, then stopped, over and again, right past a group of teenagers he barely knew. At his age, I would have dove under the seat with embarrassment. Not Kevin. He burst out laughing. He waved, beeped the horn, and kept right on jerking around the parking lot, waving and beeping every time he passed the kids. When we finished some twenty minutes later, he still didn't know how to shift. Who cares? We had fun.

Other parents may count on their kids to finish their homework on time, do the dishes, or take out the trash. I count on something better: I count on my son to make me laugh.

—*Cynthia Washam*

Crazy Gifts

My grandmother loved gardenias, Hershey bars with almonds, Joy perfume, and tall men. She cooked beef stroganoff, rack of lamb, and other hearty American fare every night for her husband and six children. Six feet tall, with a flare for eclectic fashion, a deep throaty laugh, and a slim brown cigarette burning between her fingers, she stood out wherever she went.

Her eldest daughter, my mother, grows geraniums year round on the East Coast. She knows how to cook her mother's beef stroganoff and has bested her rack of lamb. While I lived at home, my mother cooked every night for my father, my brother, and me. She is tall, not as tall as her mother, swears by Manolo Blahniks, and smoked until she was into her forties.

When my mother was a freshman in college, my grandmother overdosed on sleeping pills before her

220

two youngest children came home from school. She was rushed to the hospital where my grandfather was chief surgeon. She was in a coma for some time before recovering.

Over the course of my mother's life (and my own life), my grandmother tried to kill herself two more times and was hospitalized for her bipolar illness on many more occasions. During those times, my mother never hesitated to disrupt her schedule for an unplanned visit, never avoided the embarrassment of being seen in a psychiatric ward, and never acted in such a way as to make me, her eldest daughter, think that visiting my grandmother in a mental institution was odd or awkward. She was my grandmother, and if seeing us was beneficial to her, we went.

I remember one of our visits. My grandmother, always the gift giver, did not let the modest circumstances of her small hospital room prevent her from presenting me with a gift hidden in the palm of her hand. She handed it to me quietly, behind my mother's back, as she had done many times before. That time, it was a hard-boiled egg; another time, it could have just as easily been a folded $100 bill.

In the car afterward, my mom and I laughed.

"That's Noni," Mom said. "You can always count on her for a unique gift."

As a mother now myself, I am struck by the grace with which my mother chose to embrace my mentally ill grandmother. Having grown up under the care of a woman who was exuberant and eccentric at her best but negligent and unstable at her worst, Mom could have easily dwelled on the disappointing and challenging aspects of their relationship. But the fact that I grew up thinking that my Noni was nothing short of fabulous is evidence of my mother's authentic acceptance of her mother for who she was.

My mother consistently channeled our focus toward my grandmother's finest qualities, and transformed challenging "bipolar" moments by gently joking about them. When my grandmother snuck expensive Italian gold rings through U.S. Customs by pinning them to her brassiere, my mom said, "You can't say she doesn't have good taste." When she showed up at our house at ten in the evening in a new, blue minivan that she had been living out of with her dogs, my mom said, "At least things are never dull around here." And my favorite of Mom's Noni expressions—after she'd watched my grandmother "edit" one psychiatric ward's intake forms before she would agree to be admitted—"Well, she's a character, alright."

My mom's soft-hearted comments helped make way for me to have a positive experience with my grandmother. Rather than shield me from my grand-mother's illness and eccentricities, my mother gave me ample opportunity to know Noni and to make my own connection with her. So, to me, Noni will always be the warm, funny woman who gave me Hershey bars for breakfast, let me play dress-up with her expensive designer hats, and frequently snuck me unpredictable gifts.

When the time came for me to become a mother and my mother to become a grandmother, I was still blind to the immensity of the effort my mom made on behalf of my grandmother and me. Rather than embrace my own mother's effusive love for her new grandbaby, I'm embarrassed to say I tortured her with my short temper and exasperation.

"Mom, you can't heat the bottle in the microwave."

"No, Mom, we don't turn the TV on in the afternoon."

"Mom, she's one year old; what are you doing giving her Godiva?"

Many times, a single aggravated "Mah-ahm" communicated my pointed disapproval.

In the scope of things, the missteps I perceived her making were so small, so inconsequential, they hardly seem worthy of judgment. Yet, judge them I did . . . until, one day, I woke up.

By that time, my eldest daughter was three and my youngest was two. We were on vacation in Mexico, staying in a house overlooking the Pacific Ocean. It was one of our first big family trips. We were joined by my mom, my husband's parents, and good friends of ours who had their one-year-old son with them. Our days stretched out long and sweet, like taffy—breakfasts together in the kitchen, long afternoons taking turns playing in the pool with our girls, sunset margaritas on the deck while the "big girls" sang ring-around-the-rosy, collapsing again and again to get their new friend laughing. As my daughters made their best comedic team effort, with the sun setting on the Pacific behind them, I caught a glimpse of time. And I saw how quickly it was passing. Already, our baby girl was more than a year older than our older daughter had been when we'd conceived her little sister. Already, they were running and laughing and making jokes. And with my youngest already a toddler, we had a scant few baby months left in our young family's life.

That evening, I made two decisions: I decided we weren't done with the baby years yet and we should consider bringing a "bonus" baby into our family. And I decided not to waste any more time nit-picking and judging my mom, who by all measures is the best grandmother I know. From that moment on, I chose to make way for my own daughters' fond memories of their grandmother in every way I could.

I encouraged my mother to move out to California, which she did. Now that she's here, I try to encourage and create opportunities for her to be with my daughters, including letting them have as many sleepovers at their grandmother's as they want.

A couple of weeks ago, while driving home from my mother's house, I asked my daughters how their sleepover was.

My oldest daughter, who is now five said, "Mom, it was awesome! We had chocolate ice cream and bacon for breakfast!"

My response: "That Nonny makes a tasty breakfast!"

My mother has helped my girls amass a large collection of commercialized toys I would never buy. When she is in charge, they go to bed "pretty early" by her standards—9:30 or so. And, to carry on the family love of fashion, my mother has made sure that for all occasions, big and small, my girls are outfitted in getups that would inspire envy in Fancy Nancy. My response to it all: "Wow, Nonny sure knows how to have a good time, doesn't she!"

This is how I've chosen to do my part to ensure that the gift of grandmother love gets passed on in our family. This is how I've chosen to practice what my mother did so well, loving and accepting her own mother. And, while I am far from perfect, I do my best to follow in my mother's footsteps by focusing on what is wonderful and treating the rest with warm, accepting humor. So, these days, if you come to my house, you will see that I grow geraniums and gardenias all year long; I am a sucker for an expensive, sexy pair of shoes; and with smoking out of fashion, I pay tribute to my grandmother's and my mother's mischievous irreverence by toasting the pending arrival of baby number three with a glass of real champagne.

—*Cristina Olivetti Spencer*

A Change
in the Wind

We're in the sporting goods store to buy softball cleats. I survey the selection of shoes, turning them over to study the cleat patterns.

I ask the salesman, "Is it better to have the cleats in the middle, like this one, or just around the edge?"

My daughter is embarrassed. She doesn't roll her eyes or let out a sharp breath, but I can feel it, as if the air suddenly became five degrees cooler. It's a change in the wind.

"And which is better, rubber or plastic cleats?"

She moves a few feet away from me and starts examining the baseball socks, as if that small bit of space between us can fool everyone into thinking that she's not with me—that, at eleven years old, she is here on her own, buying long blue baseball socks.

Although she's done nothing, I get exasperated. My comment is directed toward the salesman but is meant for my daughter. "I've never bought cleats before!"

"It's okay," he reassures me and suggests a certain model, as if I were really talking about cleats.

Lately, it doesn't take much for me to embarrass her. I work at her school, in the library. When she's around her friends, she is silly, happy. I don't intrude on her there. I try not to talk to her any more than I do with any other student. When she's at the lunch table with her friends I don't go over and say "hi." Sometimes when we're going to the car, she walks a little too fast in front of me, like we're not together. I try not to take it personally, but these little rejections sometimes sting, even if I know that it's normal for her age.

One day, she race-walked into the library. She had an assignment that she had forgotten about, to interview a person whose advice had been good.

"Will you answer my questions?" she asked.

"So my advice is good?" I pressed.

"It's due in an hour! Will you answer my questions?"

I could have made her work for it, but I didn't. I believe that, even though she'd never admit it, she does think I have good advice, that she knows she can trust me.

She asked me what quotation I found inspiring, and I told her this one, by Louisa May Alcott: "I am not afraid of storms, for I'm learning to sail my ship."

It came to mind because I got it in a fortune cookie once, and I taped it to my computer monitor. Also, it's true, that quote. I don't know how to mother an adolescent daughter, to give her the space she craves and still be there when she needs me. But I'm learning because I have to captain a steady ship for her. I don't know what the waves will be like for her, but they can be rough.

Now, she's trying on the shoes. I told the salesman that she wears a five, maybe a five and a half, but she's struggling to get the five and a half onto her foot. She's writhing around with a desperate look on her face.

"It's too small!" she says miserably.

"How can that be?" I ask nobody. "Your other shoes are a five. Where is it too small?"

"All over!"

I mouth to the salesman, "A six?"

"No problem," he says cheerfully. "But that's an adult size. It will be five dollars more."

Then he turns to my daughter. "Why don't I measure your foot, kiddo?"

She winces. I wince. I know she doesn't like this man calling her "kiddo." I don't like it.

He measures her foot and it's a five and a half. There is a brief silence, as if we are all contemplating the significance of this foot that is too big to fit into the kids' shoes but not technically ready for the adult shoes.

"Well, the shoes all run differently, kiddo. I'll get a six."

The six fits, and she relaxes. Then I say something stupid.

I say: "Is it comfortable enough to run in? Do you want to run around the store?"

I don't know where that came from. Of course she doesn't want to run around the store. She would rather stick pins in the skin of her eyelids than run around the store in her new softball cleats. Her eyes widen.

"Go ahead, kiddo!" the salesman says jovially.

She shakes her head, fast, a tiny shake, more of a shudder.

I turn to the salesman. "I think we'll take these."

Back home, she tries on her new cleats. I am one inch taller than she is but not when she's wearing the cleats. She likes to wear them. She stands on her tiptoes and stretches her neck up and says, "I'm taller than you are!" and she pats my head indulgently. It's certain that I will eventually be the shortest member of our family. I am the ultimate growth chart for her. She can't wait to surpass me. It doesn't bother me, but I joke around anyway, saying that she needs to stop growing or that I'm going to put rocks on her head to slow her down. Her new height is all the more sweet for her because of my complaints.

It is bedtime, and her cleats are lined up neatly in her closet. They are arranged carefully, the one ordered thing among the chaos of her room.

I do the same thing I do every night before she goes to bed. I hug her and I don't let her go. She pushes away and I hold tighter, and then I act like she's the one holding tight. I say, "A short hug is fine. Why do you always hug so long?" and I sigh, exasperated.

She kicks her feet and moans and laughs.

Eventually, I release her and I say, "Finally! Enough is enough already!"

She always comes for that hug and she always laughs. She doesn't like going to bed until we do the hug. I think she likes pushing away from me. And I think she likes me holding on, not letting go.

—*Jody Mace*

The Best Days
of Our Lives

Today I am going to make doughnuts for my sons.

"We're going to make them?" my five-year-old responds, as if I have just announced plans to make a television. "Like, make them from ingredients?"

"Yes," I reply. "Just like my mother used to make."

I still remember those Saturday mornings when I would wake up to the clanging of pots in the kitchen cabinets downstairs. If the rattling went on for long enough, my sister and I knew that Mom was going deep into the cabinets, searching for the waffle iron or the big pot. Those were the best mornings, and they didn't happen very often.

The big pot was used only for doughnuts. At the first smell of hot grease, my sister and I would come rushing downstairs. If we were fast enough, we could help Mom with the ingredients, which consisted of two cans of white biscuit dough, a paper sack, and a box of powdered sugar. We weren't allowed to help with the oil.

Mom would hand me the biscuits to open. I'd peel the metallic paper away in a messy spiral, then bash the side of the cardboard tube against the Formica countertop's edge. They popped open with a satisfying sigh.

Meanwhile, Mom would dig through the medicine cabinet for an aspirin bottle and dump out the pills into a spoon rest by the sink. After we'd separated the biscuits and laid them on the counter, she would carefully pop the centers out of each "doughnut" with the empty bottle, making perfect wheel shapes and tiny little spheres. The holes were always our favorites.

A minute in the grease, a quick flip with the slotted spoon to fry both sides, a few minutes' rest on a paper-towel-covered plate, and the doughnuts were ready to be sugared. My sister and I would fight over who got to shake them in the bag full of powdered sugar. We'd also fight over who got to eat the first one, who got more holes, and who had to clean up.

My boys are standing in my kitchen—my fancy kitchen with its recessed lighting and slate countertops (so much harder to clean than Formica; if I had only known!). They are looking at me with expectation. I want this to be perfect, and so I do what I always do. I call my mom.

"Hello?" She sounds grumpy and slightly worried.

I think she was asleep; it *is* seven o'clock on a Saturday.

"Sorry, Mom," I apologize. "I just need a recipe."

She laughs. I have been married for eleven years, a mother for nine, and I still call her every time I attempt one of "her" recipes. Hey, I'm not that good a cook. I'll take all the help I can get. Secretly, I think she likes getting the calls.

I know I could get the information online in a minute, but I can never believe that those simple recipes are the ones that tasted so fabulous when I was a child. I mean, didn't she put something special in it? I'll ask her, something not in the recipe? Some spice, some seasoning that made it different from the swill my friends' mothers made?

"No," she usually replies. "It's just the chicken, the rice, and the can of cream of mushroom soup."

I was a vegetarian for six years. She hated that. She tells me that is the reason I'm not a natural cook—my formative cooking years were spent fiddling around with tabouleh and tofu. During this "phase," she used to sneak chicken broth into recipes that didn't call for it, just to watch me eat it. After enough years of eating vegetables alone, you can tell when there's chicken broth in your food . . . because it tastes better.

"What are you cooking today?"

"Well, I was telling the boys about my favorite breakfast when I was a kid, and I'm making that." I pause. "I bet you can guess."

"Huh? . . . Waffles?" she asks. "Don't you know how to open a box of Bisquick? The recipe's on the back."

"No, Mom. Doughnuts."

"I never made you doughnuts," she replies, confused.

What is this, a senior moment? She's only sixty-two.

"No, Mom, the ones from the little packets of biscuits. I think I have everything: powdered sugar, an Advil bottle . . ." I trail off.

She is laughing. I think she is laughing at me. "That was your favorite breakfast?" she splutters.

"Yes."

"Why?" She sounds amazed.

"Well, because you only made it on special days, so we didn't have it often, I suppose."

"Oh, sweetheart," she laughs into the phone. "I only made those doughnuts on the days when we had absolutely no money."

What? What is she talking about?

"Those biscuits only cost a nickel a can back then," she explains. "So at the end of a really bad month, when we had nothing left for food, if I could scrape up a dime, I could feed you kids."

"I hated making those doughnuts," she confesses. "Those were the worst days of my life. I used to try not to cry into the grease."

I am dumbstruck. Those mornings when my sister and I would race to the kitchen, wondering at the miracle that had brought doughnuts—homemade doughnuts (or close enough)—into our lives, those were the worst mornings of her life?

I knew we weren't well-off when I was a child. My parents both worked two jobs most of the time. Some years we got a little allowance, most years not. My mom believed that chores were character-building, and so my sister and I did the laundry, the dishes, the dusting, the vacuuming, you name it. Of course, Mom was usually working while we cleaned, teaching piano lessons in the front room to neighbor's kids, or making our play clothes at her sewing machine. (I never wanted to learn how to sew; I was convinced that if I learned how, I would be poor and have to make my children's clothing when I was an adult. I regret that decision every time I have to take a pair of pants to the tailor's to get hemmed.) I hated the homemade clothes then. They made me look different from the other kids—never a good thing—and I knew I wore them because we didn't have the money for "bought" clothes.

Sometimes, the homemade clothes made me cry; for her, it was those doughnuts.

My mom almost never cried. I mean, I know she cried a few times—that awful Mother's Day when we all forgot to get her anything, the night when Papa had the stroke. Those were some of my most frightening childhood memories, when the ground beneath my feet seemed to tremble. Mom taught me to be careful with my own tears, and how to love your children and be strong for them in the very worst times.

She is quiet on the phone; we are both remembering those days.

"Wow," I say at last, wondering if it's appropriate to make the doughnuts now that I know what they meant to her.

"How much do the biscuits cost these days?" she asks, and I realize she has probably not bought those canned biscuits since she's had enough money to avoid them.

"About fifty cents a pop," I reply. I had bought the cheapest ones, the brand she had used.

"What a rip-off!" She laughs, and everything is okay again.

She talks me through the simple steps to make them, warning me not to let the boys near the oil.

"And don't let my grandkids eat themselves sick, okay?"

I hang up, and my boys, impatient now, rush to help unroll the biscuits and pop the centers out. I drop one of the doughnut holes into my big pot full of oil, testing to see if the oil is hot enough. It is, and the little wedge of dough bobs and hisses as it cooks. My kitchen fills with the smell of doughnuts, the same kind my mother made.

I am not as good a cook as Mom was and not nearly as resourceful; I haven't had to be. But when I have moments of indecision, wondering if I am doing this right—this whole mothering thing—I stop and remember what she did, and try to get as close as possible to her special recipe.

I smile when my boys start to fight over the bag of powdered sugar, and I try as hard as I can not to cry into the grease.

—*Nikki Loftin*

Payback

The sound of laughter rings through the house as my granddaughters race from room to room. They are high on sugar cookies and anticipation. The last time we came to visit we brought them each an instrument. My husband Mike and I had decided that creative gifts were best for our grandchildren and, in this case, the louder the better. Shelly received a guitar, Rachel a drum set.

"They have practiced every day, getting ready for this performance," my son Patrick, their father, tells me.

"Payback," I respond, remembering how he used to play his guitar for hours on end, day after day, the same song over and over until I thought I would scream.

Sometimes I did.

"Turn that music *down*! I can't hear the TV!"

239

"No, you turn the sound *up* if you want to hear the TV. Or better yet, turn it off!"

Then the battle would be on—another round of what felt like a never-ending war for control of this boy. Night after night, I prayed that I would find a way to somehow reach him before he took his intelligence and his future and tossed them into the wind.

Being a parent is hard. Being a single parent, as I was then, is backbreaking, soul-wrenching, sometimes heartbreaking work. The outcome is so hard to predict, the payoff so critical. At times when my son was growing up, I was afraid I'd failed.

Once, when Patrick was fifteen, I discovered he'd been skipping school. One of the neighbors spotted him climbing the tree in our backyard and going back into the house through his bedroom window after I left for work each day. So I grounded him . . . again.

"Big deal," he told me. "If I can climb in, I can climb out. Face it, you can't hold me forever."

He was right, I couldn't hold him forever. Couldn't always steer him in the right direction. Couldn't always keep him safe. That's why I tried so hard to get through to him. The time would come when he'd really be on his own, and I wanted him to be prepared, to know where he was going.

Two weeks later, his mood had changed.

"Hey, Mom, guess what?" he smiled, wrapping his arm around my shoulders. "I'm fifteen and a half today. That means I can get my learners permit. Will you sign this for me?"

Oh no, I thought. *All I need now is to have him racing around town in a car. How can we possibly believe that adolescents are mature enough to pilot tons of machinery at high speeds through our streets?*

"You're gonna say no, aren't you? I can see it in your face." His eyes flash with anger and then dim as disappointment sets in.

And that is what got to me. I could not bear to disappoint him again. Ever since his father had left, I had been forced to say no to Patrick so many times it had almost become automatic. "No" to the latest footwear fad, "no" to a new guitar, "no" to a request for tickets to the concert—no, no, no. That's all he seemed to hear from me. That's all he had come to expect. No wonder he was sullen and withdrawn.

Not this time, I decided.

"Give me that." I grinned, taking the paper from him and reaching for a pen.

"Really?"

"Yes, really," I said. "But there have to be some ground rules. You are not to drive with anyone but me until you get your license. Once you pass the test, there will be no joyriding with your friends. You have to remember that I need this car to get to work and to keep this household afloat. You're not going to be able to use it every day. And you have to go to school. No more skipping."

"Okay. I know all that. I promise I won't bug you to drive every day. Maybe I can get a part-time job and start saving for my own car. Just sign now please, before you change your mind."

The crisp air and full moon had an energizing affect on both of us the night I took him out to the high school parking lot for his first driving lesson.

He did well for a beginner—once he got past the need to tramp down hard on the accelerator, that is. Around and around we went, circling the lot as I wondered how I was going to pay for the extra gas we were burning. Over the next several weeks, we spent many hours that way, driving in circles and easing in and out of parking spaces. Before I knew it, he was ready to hit the road for the first time.

"Here we go," he grinned, maneuvering the car into traffic.

"Home, James," I quipped, pretending he was my chauffer.

I watched as he eased his way through the streets, stopping smoothly at stop signs and red lights, signaling his turns well in advance. I began to relax my grip on the door handle.

A few moments passed before I realized we were on an unfamiliar street.

"Where are we?" I panicked. I hated being lost.

"Relax, Mom, I've got it all under control. It's the route I take when I come home from school. It takes a little longer, but it gives me time to think, and sometimes in the winter, you can see the sun set right over those trees. It's awesome."

"What do you think about?"

"Oh lots of stuff. Nothing much. It depends on the day. Sometimes I wonder what I'm gonna be when I grow up. If I'll be a dad someday and if I'll know how to do it right. Do you think I can be a musician? Do something with music?"

"You can be anything you want to be," I assured him as we pulled into the driveway.

"I sure hope so, but you gotta say that, you're my mom."

I smiled, remembering I'd said those exact words to my own mother when she'd assured me that the gap in my front teeth would eventually close and I would be pretty someday.

Things between my son and I changed after that night. Patrick had taken me down a new path, showing me not only a new route home but also a glimpse of the future. This sensitive young man with stars in his eyes and music in his soul was going to be just fine, I realized. The road might be a little rough right now and then, but he was on the right path.

"Are you ready, Grandma?" the girls ask in unison.

"I'm ready."

I can't help but laugh as Shelly takes up the microphone.

"How you all doin' tonight?" she asks. Then she and Rachel launch into one of the songs that used to drive me crazy all those years ago when my son played it on his guitar—over and over and over again.

Yes, he's done something with music, all right. He's passed his gift on to his children.

"Payback," he whispers, beaming at his two girls, both pretty, one with a gap between her front teeth.

—*Bobbi Carducci*

The Mominator

As a teenager, I found a strange picture of myself in a box of stray family memories. The photo was black and white, and I was standing outside in a short dress, no shoes on, wind blowing my blond waves. I looked to be about ten years old and was wearing the expression I saved for those special occasions when someone insisted I wear a dress and then had the nerve to take my picture. I took the photo to my mom and asked when and where it was taken.

"Let's see," she said. "I was probably about ten years old, and I was standing in the big field on your grandparents' farm."

She laughed at the horror on my face. "Don't look so panicked," she told me. "It's inevitable that you would look at least a little like me, your biological mother."

She was right. I was panicking. At that point in my life, I prided myself on being as different from my mother as was humanly possible. Different styles. Different speech. Different beliefs. Different woman. She always seemed worried about what other people thought, and I prided myself on not caring at all what other people thought. My father often referred to himself as our referee and told people that one day, when we finally stopped yelling at one another, we would realize just how alike we were. I hated when he said that and chalked it up to wishful thinking on his part—about both the cease-fire and the similarity between mother and daughter.

When I was fourteen, a school screening revealed that I had scoliosis. To avoid having a metal rod put in my back, I had to wear a corrective brace twenty-three hours a day. My mother and I had long since abandoned the idea that we could shop together without anyone getting hurt, but after I was fitted for the brace, we shelved our weapons. We spent hours shopping together, trying to find loose clothing that would hide the bulky brace from the world. Everything I wore had to have an elastic waist, so normal teenage clothing like jeans was out.

I was extremely self-conscious and even avoided hugs so that no one would feel the brace under my clothing. While other girls were worrying about how to get boys to notice them, I was worried about how to make sure boys didn't notice me. I did like a boy at our church, though, and agonized over what to wear each Sunday, furious with my oversized, matronly clothing. My mom probably suspected why I wanted a new dress for church, but she never let on. We spent an entire Saturday going from store to store, until we finally found a dress that hid the brace and looked like something a teenager would wear.

The next morning, I wore the dress to church, confident that no one could see the brace and finally feeling pretty again. After services ended, a friend whispered to me that there were small holes in the back of the dress. I was horrified. I made my mother take me home right away and tore off the dress as soon as I was safely inside my bedroom. The fabric of the dress was so thin that when I'd moved against the hard wood of the pews, the small metal attachments on the brace had worn straight through. All I wanted to do was curl up in my bed and cry.

My mom, though, was furious and insisted that we take the dress back to the store that afternoon. "We're going to get our money back and get you another dress," she told me. "They should be ashamed for selling something so cheaply made."

Reluctantly, I went with her. During the ride to the mall, I tentatively questioned how she was going to get a refund on a dress that my brace had ruined, but she refused to see the situation that way. She never once even acknowledged the role my brace had played. I had seen her angry like this before, and I knew better than to try to stop her. The woman could get a full refund on a package of chicken breasts three days after we had already digested the chicken and the mashed potatoes she'd served with it. Although I knew better than to protest, I didn't see the point in returning the dress. My life was ruined. I was a freak. What did it matter if we got the money back for the dress?

By the time we reached the mall, I was angry with my mom for being so cheap. I wondered why she just couldn't let it go. I was too embarrassed to go in the store, and she didn't press the issue.

"It's just as well," she told me. "This won't be pretty."

As I stared at her, the conservative dress she had worn to church faded away into military fatigues and the department store bag morphed into a bazooka. Striding away from the car, she became Arnold Schwarzenegger in *The Terminator*. I fully expected her to turn around and say, "I'll be back."

Sure enough, when she came back out, she had a full refund in hand. Terrified shoppers and store clerks had fled the building moments before she appeared, and smoke was rising from the dress department as we pulled away.

For a long time, I thought of that dress as another example of my mom being scary and cheap. But that day I was glad she was scary and cheap, because I felt vindicated. Score one for the girl in the back brace.

It was only after I had two sons of my own that I realized the return of that dress had nothing to do with my mom being scary or cheap and everything to do with how much she loved me. What I had needed most at that moment was to feel like any other girl, and my mom had fought for that.

Shortly after my younger son turned two, his name was added to a waiting list to see a specialist in developmental disorders at a children's hospital. Six months later, he was diagnosed as being within the autistic spectrum, which meant that he had some characteristics consistent with autism but had other characteristics consistent with other disorders or with traditionally developing children. After we got the diagnosis, I did a lot of reading. Over and over, the experts said that parents of kids with any type of disability or disorder need to take time to grieve for the child they thought they had—for the "normal" child their child could not be. Although I understood this idea, I rejected it. I was too worried about what life would be like for my son to worry about any sense of loss on my own part.

I began taking him to a center for children with disabilities shortly after his diagnosis. Many of the children in his group had multiple diagnoses, both physical and mental. In a room filled with children who couldn't control their physical movements, my silent son seemed like the "normal" one. With no obvious physical disabilities, Josh seemed like any other three-year-old to the untrained eye. After dropping him off that first day, I cried for hours. I thought I had seen a glimpse of his future, spent in rooms filled with kids whose lives were filled with struggle.

Now, eight years later, I can see that this vision of my son's life was somewhat accurate. Josh has been to speech therapy, occupational therapy, social learning groups, and psychological counseling. Since his diagnosis, there has not been a time in his life when he wasn't seeing someone for something. However, he is also in an integrated classroom at school, where kids with and without disabilities learn together.

I have had to struggle between wanting my son to be treated "normally" and acknowledging that treating him like the other kids can also do him a grave disservice. Josh has little concept of appropriate social behavior; his actions are often more consistent with a much younger child. People typically judge him to be weird or rude, not realizing that he has any type of disorder.

Josh has had some really great teachers and some not-so-great teachers. He is on an Individualized Educational Plan (IEP) that outlines goals for his education and details what special services he can receive. Because he is so smart, we occasionally run across someone who just doesn't buy into his IEP or his diagnosis—who sees Josh as odd and undisciplined but not meriting any kind of special help.

A few years ago, Josh had a teacher who rejected the idea that he needed special attention. I have always hated labels, but I knew that, in Josh's case, I had to fight for the label if my son was to get the help he needed. I found myself in the utterly unenviable position of fighting for my son to be treated differently. I prepared for the annual meeting to revise his IEP by researching other plans, talking to developmental specialists, and quizzing other parents of kids with similar disorders.

A few days before the meeting, I called my mom and asked if she would come to the meeting with me.

She didn't ask me why I wanted her to come. She just asked, "What time?"

It seems strange that walking into a room with tiny plastic chairs would be intimidating, but that day, walking into that IEP meeting, I felt the full weight of my son's future on my shoulders. It was the first time I truly had to fight for my son to be treated according to his disorder. Part of me just wanted to forget the whole thing, to find a way to help Josh get through school without insisting that the school acknowledge he was different. But I couldn't just forget it, because it was a question of what my son needed. I took a deep breath in the doorway of that IEP room and found myself remembering my mom that day in the parking lot, my mom telling me, "This won't be pretty," and marching into that department store with the ruined dress.

My mom sat in the IEP meeting with me, and although she didn't say a word, I knew she was shooting invisible death rays from her eyes the entire time. I'm glad she was there, fighting for me again. Glad that she showed me how loving a child means fighting for what they need, even if you sometimes appear scary and cheap to the untrained eye. Terrified teachers and schoolchildren may not have fled the building ahead of me and smoke may not have been coming from that IEP room as I pulled away, but, with the revised IEP on the seat next to me, I felt like my mom coming back to the car with the full refund.

These days, I teach at a public university where many of my students are graduates of the high school where my mom teaches. Sometimes, just for fun, I'll ask these graduates if they know Mrs. Brewster, and then I'll laugh at their amazed expressions when I reveal that Mrs. Brewster is my mom. After a few moments, they nod and say, "I can see that." And I'm glad they can.

Finally, so many years later, I realize what my dad meant so long ago when he insisted my mother and I were so much alike. In a way, I am that girl in the black and white picture. And I'm thankful. Death rays are very useful weapons for mothers.

—Andrea Harris

When Autumn Comes

On Lake Odessa, I watch the mallards swim up and bob for food, their small heads underwater, tail feathers standing upright. It is late September, and I am here with a group of women friends for a writing retreat. We are sharing stories about our lives.

As I sit by the window with an open journal in my lap, the antics of the mallards take me back to when my daughter was still a little girl. We lived in the Upper Peninsula of Michigan in Marquette, and I often took Senara on long walks. Down at Lower Harbor, we dropped bits of bread or corn kernels into the water and laughed as the ducks scrambled to gather the pieces into their bills. On other days, we drove to Presque Isle, past tall Lombardy poplar trees lining Lakeshore Boulevard, and walked into the island woods, Senara holding my hand. We gathered leaves from sugar maples, red oaks, and white birches, tucking them into our pockets along with acorns and pinecones. We named each leaf a different color—kettle-bottom bronze, bread-crust brown, candy-corn orange—until we ran out of metaphors.

By the end of September in Northern Michigan, the air would have already turned crisp with the coming winter's first chill. Life was simple then. I was learning to be a single mother and, contrary to the traditional wisdom, finding it surprisingly easy.

Senara at four and then five bounded through life full of energy, long light curls flying, dark eyes so much like my own. In the woods, breathing in that loamy smell of damp earth, Senara listened for the ovenbird's call, *teacher-teacher-teacher*, or the red-eyed vireo chirping *look up, up here*. Sometimes, I told her, "Be quiet, very quiet," and we waited for the white-throated sparrow. "Listen," I told her, and we heard its plaintive whistle for *old Sam Peabody, Peabody, Peabody*.

I taught her to move softly on the pine-needle carpet, her small feet pressing moss and dried leaves gently—the way Native Americans stepped in their moccasins long ago. If we were lucky, over the next steep bank we'd find a white-tailed doe and her spring-born young foraging for food. The deer were so tame we could almost put out our hands to touch their warm, sleek coats.

I showed her a striped maple, pointed out its greenish bark, and large three-lobed leaves. "My dad called this snakewood," I told her.

Even as a little girl, she used to say, "I wish I knew your dad."

My parents died long before her birth, my father when I was only sixteen.

"What were your parents like?" she often asked.

My mother was sometimes sad, I wanted to tell her, but when she was happy our house smelled like vanilla and lilacs. Instead, I said, "She sang songs with me. She made up silly words. Sometimes, we harmonized and laughed when we came down off high notes. I loved to sing with my mother."

"My dad loved nature," I told her. "He took me for walks in the woods and we'd pick thimbleberries for jam. Once, he put my hand over the black bark of the hemlock so I could feel the soft green lichen growing over it. We stood like that for a long time.

"In the spring," I went on, "we looked for the first white trillium and pink lady's slipper. He told me about floating down the Mississippi River, working on an iron ore boat, sailing across Lake Huron. He lived in Louisiana for a while, ran a restaurant there. He always talked about the jazz bands of New Orleans, the taste of hot gumbo, and the smell of magnolia blossoms. 'Nothing in the world smells sweeter than the magnolia blooms,' he said."

"I think I'd like your dad," Senara said.

"Yes, and he'd have loved you so much," I said. "He always wanted to be a grandfather."

This seems far in the past now—our simple walks, her growing up. Now, she is thirteen.

This summer we took out the old photos, looked through them, and there she was, only two, tucked in the Lands' End backpack. In the photo, I am bending over so Senara can offer a young deer some corn kernels. She is laughing as the deer licks her tiny fingers before she lets go of the corn.

"I think I remember this," she said.

I wonder, though, how much a young child truly recalls. Was it her real memory or the memory of the stories we have repeated?

Sometimes, I fear that she remembers her dad and me fighting, the raised voices, slammed doors, the time I chased his truck down the driveway when he strapped her in her car seat, threatening to take her away from me. I hope she has forgotten that.

Senara's preteen years were hard for us. We argued often, not the usual arguments about clothes or friends, because I trusted her judgment and I have taught her to be careful and open-minded. We argued about her going to live with her dad.

"You've had me for years," she said. "Now it's his turn."

In the summer, she always goes camping with her dad, floats down the Escanaba River in a canoe, hikes to Trapper's Falls in the Porcupine Mountains. This is what I did with my dad, hiking, fishing, hunting for rocks. My dad taught me to drive our old Chevy Biscayne on country roads when I was fourteen. He was my partner in crime. Once, we put on snowshoes, plowed through the woods looking for wolves, following tracks of an ephemeral animal we never found. We kept many of these exploits a secret from my mother.

Senara's dad loves her. The first and only time I ever saw him cry was when we moved to Kansas to be closer to the man who would eventually become my husband. Senara, then only five, played her Walkman all though Michigan, Illinois, and Missouri, listening to the love song from the movie *Titanic* over and over.

This summer, after many disagreements, I decided to let Senara live the school year with her father and her stepmother up north. As I sit and watch the ducks swim across Lake Odessa, I realize this will be the first autumn we won't go to the Country Mill to drink apple cider, hunt for the plumpest pumpkin, and eat sugary cinnamon-covered donuts in the tourist-packed picnic area. We won't decorate our front porch with the ghost we made when she was seven, the gangly skeleton we bought at Wal-Mart, and the blinking pumpkin lights.

Last year, Senara banned me from trick or treating for the first time. Dressed as a rap singer, she roamed the neighborhood and gathered treats in a pillowcase with her friends. I knew then she was growing up. I took our dog, Spencer, for a walk, feeling lonely among all the parents still holding their youngsters' hands as they coaxed them to approach a house and ring the doorbell. "Trick or treat," "Trick or treat," called in a cacophony of childish voices. I passed all our favorite homes decorated for the season. Even the dog seemed sad to lose his little companion. I stopped at the display off Scott Street, the house with its whole backyard turned into a cemetery with a motorized spider and talking zombie. The crowd of parents and screaming children jostled me, and Spencer tugged at his leash, wanting to move on.

I knew this day was coming—when I would have to let go, when it was time to allow her to make more of her own decisions and trust that I have taught her many good values, ones that will help her as she travels on without me. The poet Kahlil Gibran once wrote something about your children never truly belonging to you, about having them for a little while before they leave home to find their own way. I just never thought it would happen so soon. Senara still has four years of high school and numerous occasions I will miss during the school year, such as teasing her while she gets ready for her first official date, cheering for her to run faster at a track meet, and snapping pictures as she poses in her senior prom dress. I may be able to be there for some of these big events, but for most of them, time, miles, and work commitments will interfere.

But I don't want to make her feel guilty for leaving, because I know that will make her push me away. I used to hate it when my mother made me feel guilty about something I said or did.

Every night, Senara calls me to tell me about her day, the new friends she is making, her French and drama classes. She misses her friends back home, and I know she misses me. Occasionally, she fights with her stepmother. She is learning life is not always so easy. She has to work harder, take on more responsibility. Sometimes, I know, I was too easy on her. I didn't always set limits for her or at least not always the right ones.

She bought a circle journal, and last week she sent me her first entry, with pictures of her school, her friends, and the horse on which she is taking riding lessons.

She wrote, "Mom, I forgot it gets so cold up north, even in September. I forgot how the early morning frost turns your breath into white smoke and rushes into your lungs until it hurts to breathe."

I believe she has inherited my poetic talent.

I will write back, tell her about this weekend at the lake, my students at the community college, how difficult it is to teach argumentative writing. I don't think I will mention the cider mill, because I probably won't drive out there this year. The front porch of our house may end up less a jack-o'-lantern. Senara always helped me carve it; only she can carve the scariest faces. She's been scooping out the seeds since she was seven. Then again, maybe I will find a jack-o'-lantern to illuminate the porch on Halloween Eve.

Out on Lake Odessa, the mallards rise and fly away. Overhead, a V-formation of honking geese begins their journey to a warmer season. I pick up my pen and write to Senara, "Today is the first day of autumn."

—*Rosalie Sanara Petrouske*

Just to Be with You

"All I want to do is just to be with you, be with you . . ."

The song lyrics, from my daughter's *High School Musical 3* CD, filled our SUV as my husband, two daughters, and I left our suburban Ohio home and headed one hour south toward my mom's 200-year-old dairy farm.

"Play that song again!" my eldest daughter begged from the backseat.

As the vistas transformed from malls and coffee shops to silos and cornfields, we sang our hearts out, echoing words from a teenage love song that seemed strangely appropriate for this day. "All I want to do is just to be with you . . ."

Usually, we *were* together on Sundays, feasting on my husband's homemade pancakes and then piling into the car to attend worship services and Sunday school. But today, I wanted more, and I didn't want to come home to the usual scene—homework hassles, piano practice sessions, and a litany of motherhood worries. *What if my first grader's runny nose turns into a sinus infection? What if my nine-year-old never finishes her book report?* At lunch time I didn't want to tear the crusts off two peanut butter and jelly sandwiches, one with grape jelly, one with strawberry. I didn't want to sweep away crumbs or salty tears. Selfishly, I wanted to receive, not give.

I knew just who to call. "Hi, Mom. Can we come over for Sunday dinner?"

My mother's farmhouse, cozy with smells of cinnamon and apples, welcomed us from a frigid February snowstorm. As we peeled off layers of boots and coats, a layer of worry seemed to shed from my very core. While my daughters bounced around, ripping open Mom's offering of markers and colored paper, I sat down, shrugging my shoulders at their antics.

"I have plastic to cover the table while they color," Mom said, following my concerned eyes as they traveled to her white lace tablecloth.

Her voice, quiet and comforting, was the same one that reassured me in sixth grade when I was picked last for the kickball team and was ridiculed for having pristine, white gym sneakers.

"Just remember that everyone at home loves you so much," she told me in the car that day after school. "Then you can get through anything."

"Can I help?" I offered, watching as Mom and her husband spooned steamy mashed potatoes into a serving bowl.

"No, you just sit," Mom instructed.

She placed a platter of breaded pork chops on the table—my very favorite meal, the one I requested for each and every childhood birthday. Suddenly, I was a child again, filling up on my mother's love and devotion.

Although I didn't grow up on the dairy farm, today, my mom's log cabin farmhouse felt like home—safe, fun, and overflowing with love.

"Want to play I Spy?" Mom asked the girls after they finished the last of their homemade apple pie and ice cream.

Giggles spilled from the living room as my daughters searched for hidden "treasure": a gold tin filled with cotton balls that Mom hid behind the furniture. As the girls played, I indulged in a second cup of freshly brewed coffee.

"Can we go out to the barn?" I asked later, like a child needing a permission slip.

We tromped through the snow, surprising a few cats with our arrival. In her blue jeans and rubber boots, Mom led the way, her hasty gait revealing her love of the outdoors but never giving away her age (seventy-something) or her struggles with osteoporosis. As we stopped in the barn, a Jersey cow leaned its head over the gate, desperate to nuzzle Mom's jacket. I understood. It felt good to be close to unconditional love.

"Can we come here in the summer, Grandma?" My girls, dizzy from chasing a tiger cat in circles, stopped to catch their breath.

"You're welcome here any time."

Guilt crept forward as I remembered our last farm visit. Had it been a full year ago? Mom had visited our house for Christmas, but why hadn't we taken time to travel her way? Had silly worries like homework, piano practice, and laundry taken precedence over spending time with my own mother?

"We were thinking about coming for Easter dinner," I said sheepishly. "I could bring a salad."

"Great!" Mom grinned. "But don't bring a thing."

Later, as we packed up the SUV and said our goodbyes, I didn't worry that it was nearing dusk or that the girls would miss baths and bedtimes. Though the roads were icy, I felt strangely safe. As we turned onto the freeway, I knew exactly what CD to play: "All I want to do is just to be with you . . ."

"We'll be back again soon," I promised the girls. Through the darkened car, I'm pretty sure I saw them smile.

—Stefanie Wass

Rings

We call my mother when I am in labor.

"Tell her she has to come this weekend," I instruct Kip from the hospital bed.

"Jean wants to know if you can come this weekend."

"No," I correct him. "Tell her she must take Friday off and come this weekend."

In the end, she can get only that afternoon off, so she won't get from Utah to Colorado until Friday night. I'm irritated that a stupid, long-term sub job gets priority over the birth of her first grandchild. And me.

When I was twenty-two, my siblings and I bought her a mother's ring. Five stones: emerald, ruby, garnet, rose zircon, green tourmaline. Jean, Rebecca, Katie, Jake, Barry. She wore it on her hand in place of the half-carat diamond she'd put back in its box a year earlier—unsure of what to do with it now that my father was part of a different state, different religion, different lifestyle. What do you do with a large diamond, with a twenty-three-year history, with five children and two dogs?

When she arrives, she's brought my memory box—my old teddy bear, the Cabbage Patch doll she made me, yellow and green afghans, the clothes I wore when I was small.

My newborn son, Mark, sits at my breast, detached, blowing milky breath onto the wet nipple. I watch his face. I tell her it amazes me how much it can change—the lips pulling down into a frown, then circling around into a tiny O; the folds of skin creasing inward like his face wants to crack; the way his eyebrows shoot up as if he is a very old man; how the corner of his mouth reaches up into a toothless half smile against my chest. She tells me how she used to watch my expression for hours. She tells me people used to come up to her in stores and ask if they could pet my dandelion hair.

She pulls a red jumper out of the memory box and tells me that this is the outfit I'm wearing in the picture where I stand in the sink with a bottle of cleanser.

Mark sleeps, and she empties the memory box onto the floor of his room.

"I'm out of practice," Mom says, wrapping the diaper deftly and firmly around Mark's waist.

Kip and I inspect the diaper like she has just performed a bit of magic. We have not yet been able to produce more than a sad, sagging thing, crooked, loose at his hips and tight around the legs. Hers is a masterpiece, a well-crafted piece of remembered experience.

I think about the summer Barry was born, and then two days later Bec, Jake, and I got the chicken pox, and then two weeks later we moved from Pennsylvania to Ohio. I think of my mother packing our house into neat boxes and making us chocolate chip milkshakes because the chicken pox lined our lips and mouths and throats. When school started I wrote about it in my "What I Did for Summer Vacation" paper. To my eleven-year-old mind, it was funny. I hadn't realized then what it meant for a body to have a baby—the first few days of heavy blood; the vulva that swells so that sitting, standing, and walking are painful; the hemorrhoids; the hormonal shifts; the sore nipples; the sleeplessness. I hadn't realized what it meant to pack a household into neat brown boxes while the body feels all that or how it would be to do it without the help of a too-busy husband and with children underfoot. I didn't think one single time, when I asked for another milkshake with extra chocolate chips or complained about taking a baking soda bath, that she might have been tired or sad or in pain. When I think about it now, that June grows incomprehensible to me.

In the morning, I drag to the room where Mom is staying. "Take him. Kip and I have to get some sleep."

She lies on her back on the air mattress. Mark curls up on her chest, his legs and arms tucked under him, like he hasn't yet realized he's left the warmth of a mother.

The night before my wedding, I slept with Mom in her bed. I don't remember why. I suppose there were too many siblings in other beds. Or perhaps it was just comfortable and warm and safe—like a womb—her patting my arm and back as I shifted sleeplessly through the night.

Mom: able to let me go, to give me to a man—three daughters in three years. Mom: strong enough to push me out of herself, to give me over to someone else to be weighed, measured, swaddled, and taken away.

I kept my own ring on that night—something small but dense that I could close my hand on and feel—something compact and heavy, like a solid foreign coin—something to remind me that betrayal and abandonment would not creep into our lives like they had with her and Dad.

Dad proposed by baking a check into a cake. For months, he'd been telling Mom he was going to the library to study while he was working a third job on the sly to make enough money for a ring. He dug feces out of clogged pipes so she could have a diamond bigger than he could afford. Mom bought herself a round, deep stone looped with gold and attached to a thin band.

We used to play with Dad's wedding band. I remember sitting in church and embossing rings onto my palm with it. Mom says that's how it got lost; he let us play with it in the car once and then it was gone, out the window she supposed.

She'd kept her wedding ring on always—when she washed the dishes, slept, showered. She kept it on through Dad's medical school, through all of our births, through Dad's failed business dream, through all the things that would have made other women take it off. She kept it on so long that, when the divorce proceedings began, she was worried it wouldn't slide over the widened knuckle and she'd have to have it cut off.

My mother is brave and certainly strong. It's something I do not envy. Because only experience can grant it. I want the right to be just a little fragile, a little bit "girly," a little bit less than the superwoman Mom was expected—and later forced, through divorce—to become.

The year Barry turned ten was the year Dad became obsessed with the Internet, the year he started sleeping with other people. Mom told me that, until that year, the worst year of her life had been a long time ago—when she'd had the first of a series of miscarriages, gotten pregnant again, and then miscarried the second child on the day the first was supposed to be born.

Three years after my father's first infidelity, Kip proposed to me by slipping a ring onto my finger while I lay with my eyes closed next to him on a picnic blanket. That night we went to Mom's house with the announcement.

She said something like, "Oh, that's nice."

After Kip was gone, I accused her of not being happy for me.

She told me she had expected the proposal— that's why she wasn't more excited, because it wasn't a surprise. I hoped I believed her.

Mom cuddles Mark upstairs while Kip and I stay down in the kitchen and pay bills.

By the fridge, Kip puts his arms all the way around my middle and laughs, saying, "Hey, they fit."

It feels divine.

Before I was engaged, before I was even quite sure that I wanted to be, I used to go into Mom's room and try on her boxed wedding ring, admire the shape of my hands and nails and how well it all looked with that ring. I used to imagine how, if my father was dead instead of divorced, she might have given the ring to me, passed it down to her eldest daughter. And sometimes I wished my father dead instead of divorced. Not for the ring. But because we could have grieved and recovered instead of having to readjust and reevaluate our lives. Because it wouldn't have been something we had to forgive every time a new sting arose as a result of his choices—when Mom can't find a job because of her age and inexperience; when she tells me about this dance she went to and how a weird guy named Floyd kept asking her to dance, and it's like she's fourteen again; when at night I can feel the heat from Kip's body beside me but can't fill the space between us, because we've disagreed about something and it seems that if I press too close, if I give too much, he will leave me.

Religiously, I believe in love and marriage through eternity. There is no "Till death do us part" in our wedding ceremonies. We believe in a ring of husbands and wives, brothers and sisters, sealed forever. But we also do not believe in forcing people to stay in the circle; so sometimes people choose to step out, break the band, which is what happens with a divorce.

I've always hated those wedding rings that come as part of a set—the ones that don't make a full circle, that leave a little gap where the two tips of metal don't quite meet. They make them that way so a diamond engagement ring can be fitted in. Practical and stylish and devoid of the symbol that's so important to me.

Sunday morning, Mom sits on the bed. I sit across from her in the rocking chair with Mark on my lap. She has to leave after lunch to make the drive back to Utah before she gets too tired. My first child, and I've had Mom for only forty-one hours. It cuts a sadness into me, an envy for friends whose mothers come for weeks and sometimes longer, friends with unbroken families, with nonworking mothers.

She calls me that night when she gets home and tells me she's tired but well. She also tells me Jake's car is on the fritz, so she'll have to share her car with Jake so he can get to work. That means she won't be able to come again in a couple of weekends like I'd hoped she would. She's sorry. I tell her it's fine, that I understand. But I don't.

Without her nearby, I learn to nurse and diaper, to cook and garden. And in the children I continue to have, in the cross-country moves, the financial stress, the quiet successes and intimate moments with my family, I feel myself coming more closely to my mother. I had wanted her presence, her time, her advice. Instead, she gave me a little push into the darkness, and, while my circle of trials has not included divorce or miscarriage, I have learned to face the losses that have come. In this I have learned what she has always tried to teach me in word, action, and set-jaw stubborn faith: that I can succeed, and will. This she has always believed, this I am trying to learn, this I am hoping to give my own children: a ring of love and belief in their strengths and capabilities, as beautiful and binding as their circle of soft faces when they surround me, smiling.

—*Jean Knight Pace*

Hates Kids

I stared, slack-jawed, at the artwork of my eight-year-old son, Norman. A magazine rendering of Norman Rockwell's *The Babysitter* had been crookedly cut and pasted onto white construction paper. The young woman depicted in the famous print sits holding a squalling baby on her lap while she consults a guide for babysitters. The squalling infant has a fistful of her hair, and the scowl on the babysitter's face says she wishes she were somewhere else. Beneath the slightly askew picture, my son had penned: "My mom hates kids."

Norman fidgeted at my side, watching his classmates tug their parents around the classroom, as I continued to simply gawk at his artwork. My son's picture stood apart from the more cheerful offerings of his peers. Colorful drawings of families, complete with pets and flowers blooming in the yard, all surrounded *The*

Babysitter. Captions announced everything from, "My mom's a good cooker," to "My dad takes me camping."

Mrs. Brown, Norman's third-grade teacher, paused next to me, smiling at her students' art exhibit. "I thought Norman really captured the theme of the assignment," she said.

"Assignment?" My gaze was still locked on the words "hates kids."

"Yes. I asked the children to create a picture that represents their family. Norman managed to find a woman struggling with a baby."

"I don't have a baby. Norman's eight and Derrick's seven."

"Yes, but as I understand it, Derrick's disabled and I believe Norman sees him as needing the same attention as a baby."

I turned toward Mrs. Brown, a tidy fortyish woman who'd undoubtedly witnessed the challenges of many parents.

"You're a single mother with a child who requires special care," she continued, "while Norman sees himself as fairly self-reliant."

"But I don't hate kids," my voice faltered as I blinked back tears.

"Of course you don't, but I'm guessing there are times when you hate the struggle of being a single parent of a child with special needs."

I stared at Mrs. Brown as if she'd morphed into a mirror reflecting my life. Being single, not to mention the mother of a child with a disability, hadn't been part of my fantasy growing up. As a little girl, I'd dreamed of marrying the love of my life, having two kids, a boy and a girl, and living in a house with a dog, a cat, and a white picket fence. I had hoped to be one of the families in the drawings on the classroom wall.

After Derrick's birth, a different reality set in. At nine months, Derrick's doctors determined he suffered from myriad afflictions, including cerebral palsy and mental retardation. Derrick's autism diagnosis would come a few years later, but my marriage did not survive that first year of adjusting to the demands of a child with special needs. The family of my childhood dreams had been replaced by a new family—one that required me to juggle many roles. I was the doting caregiver and the strict disciplinarian; a nursemaid and a cleaning lady; a working mom who lived on determination and creative financing.

The cacophony of excited chatter brought me back to Norman's classroom, and I noticed he had found his way across the classroom to talk to a couple of buddies. As I watched him, mischief danced in his dark brown eyes as he shared something funny with his friends. I thought of Norman as a shy boy. At home, he didn't seek out the neighborhood kids; instead, he acted more like the man of the house. Clearly, though, I realized, he had no trouble relating to other children.

I shifted my attention from Norman back to *The Babysitter*, concentrating on the young woman's scowl. Did I present that same frustrated face to my boys? Had I become a harried mother who didn't take time to show how much she loved her sons? A realization jolted me like someone had thrown cold water in my face. I needed to make a change . . . and I needed to make it now.

Managing a one-parent household and caring for two sons, especially when one is disabled, left little time for the softer things in life. Our nights were filled with quick, inexpensive dinners, Norman's home-work, two hurried baths, and simple dessert, before we all fell into bed. Day after day, we followed the same rushed routine. There never seemed to be time to sit and read my boys a bedtime story or to watch a favor-ite program on television. Weekends were less hectic, but still, laundry needed to be done, groceries bought, and bills paid. I seemed to never have the time or the money for a matinee or a trip to the zoo. I barely even managed a free day at the park.

At the time Norman made the "hates kids" col-lage, I'd been single for five years. While I couldn't go back in time to correct my parenting mistakes, I certainly could change my actions in the future. I could be a better mom from now on!

Over the next two years, I focused on activities that Norman enjoyed: baseball, basketball, soccer. If I didn't serve as team mom, I sometimes helped coach and I never missed a game. When I removed Norman's responsibility for watching Derrick as they played outside, he had the opportunity to play with the other kids in our apartment complex. I became a better planner and structured my days to allow for a story before bed. More efficient weekends afforded us family time at the park or the luxury of an occasional movie. Of course, it meant that I had more demands on my time than hours in the day. So, although my house might not have been the cleanest or the most organized, both of my sons seemed to flourish in the chaos.

Norman's third-grade year progressed through autumn and winter, and he seemed to change with the passing seasons. One warm spring night, Norman came in for dinner and launched into a story about Quan, a boy from our apartment complex, and his family, occasionally throwing in a strange word.

"What nationality is Quan?" I asked.

"Um . . ." I could see the wheels turning in his head. "He's one of those -eses. You know Chinese, Japanese. I don't remember which one."

It turned out the family had moved to Oregon from Vietnam. Norman and Quan became fast friends, spending every afternoon after school together and weekends and then the summer plotting to overtake the designated battlefield in our small backyard.

The following Thanksgiving, Norman came to me with a special request. "Mom, do you think you could teach Quan's mom how to cook a turkey?"

"Probably. Why?"

"His family wants to eat a real Thanksgiving dinner. I told her you'd help her cook it."

Norman and I met with Quan's mom, a petite woman who didn't speak a word of English. With Quan translating, I helped his mom make a grocery list and we set a time to meet Thanksgiving morning to put the turkey in the oven. Quan's mom thanked me for my help and invited us to Thanksgiving dinner. We had been planning to eat at my aunt's, but I could see how important it was to Norman that we accept her invitation. In keeping with our family's tradition, I volunteered to make the pumpkin pies.

Thanksgiving Day, after we put Quan's family's bird in the oven, I returned to my apartment and set to the task of baking pies. A sleepy-eyed Norman wandered into the kitchen as I placed the necessary ingredients on the counter.

"Can I lick the bowl?" he asked the age-old question of baking parents everywhere.

"Only if you help make the pies." I smiled at him.

Since I made pumpkin pies every year, one would think I'd have the recipe memorized. But that was not the case. The basic recipe had been taken from the back of a Libby's pumpkin pie-filling can, and over the years, several changes had been made. The amount of some ingredients had been increased or decreased; some ingredients were eliminated and some were replaced.

"Mom, why do you need all these spices when you use pumpkin pie spice? Isn't that enough?" Norman asked, as the measuring spoonful of nutmeg in his hand hovered over the bowl.

"I guess because I like to spice things up."

I mimed dumping the contents of the measuring spoon. He obliged, dumping it into the mixture, and I handed him the bottle of crushed cloves.

Like the pumpkin pie recipe, Norman, Derrick, and I had also gone through a transformation. While Libby's original formula made a delicious pie, our version incorporated ingredients that added a touch more spice and created its own unique flavor. Similarly, our once "traditional" family had experienced a few changes along the way—some rewarding, some challenging, but all adding a little spice to our lives and combining to make our own version of family.

An hour later, Norman stood holding the cooled pumpkin pie while I snapped a picture. His proud smile clearly said he'd enjoyed the pie-baking experience, and I now had a photo of our creation to accompany *The Babysitter* artwork in my box of memorabilia.

With Norman carrying the pumpkin pie and leading the way, we trudged across the apartment complex in a cold November rain. When we arrived at Quan's apartment, the boys and I removed our shoes and filed through the door. I was taken aback by the low table that had been set for dinner and was surrounded by pillows. Derrick, however, was nonplussed, and he promptly laid down, his head on a pillow and his sock-covered feet on the table.

"No, Derrick," I said, color warming my cheeks. "You sit on the pillow."

Norman and Quan plopped onto theirs, and Norman rolled his eyes at Derrick, who flashed an impish grin.

Spicy spring rolls replaced the traditional relish plate of black olives and dill pickles, and chopsticks lay next to our dishes. I snatched Derrick's away before he turned the table into a drum set. Quan's mother brought my sons and me forks, and we all dug into the holiday meal, filling our stomachs with roasted turkey and all the trimmings. Then, pride filled me as Norman and I served our pumpkin pie.

Norman had sensed how important it was for Quan's mom to create a holiday memory for her family. A family complete with a mom, a dad, a brother, and a sister. A family not that different from ours. A family still guided by traditional Vietnamese values, but adapting to change and embracing the culture of their new homeland.

In the years to come, as Norman and I navigated life's journey, I had many occasions to recall the image of *The Babysitter* and those stark words written in a child's hand. I knew all along that I didn't hate kids; I had, however, hated some of life's challenges.

I would survive the soul-wrenching decision to place Derrick in assisted-living when his care became too much me. Norman would teach me a whole new meaning to the phrase "wait until he's a teenager" as I nudged him toward a high school diploma. And I would resort once again to creative financing as I helped Norman work his way through college.

The changes I made as a result of eight-year-old Norman's now infamous rendering of *The Babysitter* came to fruition at a going-away party before he moved out of state for a new job. Norman gave a speech in which he thanked me for always being there, for always being supportive, for helping him realize his dreams. For being a great mom. Norman Rockwell couldn't have painted a more perfect picture of a mom who loved her kids.

—*Kimila Kay*

Love Blind

Charlie is six and all boy. He is a whirlwind of male energy: a maker of Lego spaceships, a transformer of innocuous sticks into laser guns, and an aficionado of toilet humor. So I was momentarily taken aback when he told me that his one wish was for a baby doll. But I am not one to force-fit my kids into gender roles; besides, taking care of a doll is good training for when he is a father someday. He could learn a lot.

Charlie didn't want just any baby doll. He wanted Baby Annabel, who is, he quoted from the Saturday morning commercial, "Incredibly lifelike! Realistic in every way!"

I was wary of the "realistic in every way" thing, because there are certain aspects of realistic baby-hood that I'm in no hurry to revisit: spit-up, changing diapers, colic, 3:00 A.M. fevers. But once I ascertained that Baby Annabel wasn't realistic in those particular ways, I bought him the doll.

She is completely predictable, which, after two unpredictable babies of my own, I appreciate. She comes with an instruction manual, which spells out exactly why she cries and what the remedy is. If you do precisely as you're told, Baby Annabel will be a happy baby. There's none of this "maybe she's hungry," "maybe she's wet," "maybe she wants to be jiggled and have monkey noises made at her" like you get with a real baby.

When Baby Annabel cries, it means she's hungry and you need to feed her with the bottle. Thankfully, no actual liquid comes out of the bottle, so there are no diapers to change.

But once she is sated, she starts to cry again.

"It's because she has to burp," Charlie explains.

I pick up Baby Annabel, lean her against my shoulder, and pat her on the back.

"Not like that!" Charlie says, shocked at how little I know about baby care.

He lays Baby Annabel on her back and performs a maneuver that is almost exactly the same as the chest compressions I learned in infant CPR class. He pushes down on her stomach several times with enough force to dislodge any object that might be stuck in her windpipe.

"Charlie!" I object. "That's not how you burp a baby!"

A burp emanates from Baby Annabel's angelic face, followed by a satisfied, "*Aaaaaahhhh.*"

Charlie looks at me just a little bit smugly and holds Baby Annabel tenderly as she drifts off to blissful sleep.

I notice something strange about Baby Annabel.

"Did you notice," I ask Charlie, "that one eye never closes when she sleeps?"

"Yes," he explains, "that is Spooky Eye."

I tell my husband, Stan, that Baby Annabel has Spooky Eye, and he endeavors to repair her. The right eye is sunken into her head, looking slightly up, as if she is having a mild seizure. The kitchen table becomes the operating table, and Stan digs a screwdriver into her eye socket, trying to pop the eyeball out a little bit.

I hover around, offering helpful advice. "What if you do this operation where you stick a bent clothes hanger through the mouth and poke the eye out from behind?"

I watch a lot of medical shows on TV and that's where I come up with many of my good ideas, but this one is all my own. In any case, there is no way to get at the back of the eye through the mouth. We don't know much about the inner anatomy of Baby Annabel's head and that makes surgery complicated.

"Can't you unscrew her head?" I ask.

But the head does not come off. Just like a real baby, her head is permanently affixed to her neck.

Stan turns on our son. "It's because he's been too rough with her."

I leap to Charlie's defense. "He hasn't been rough with her at all!"

As I say this, scenes from the past two weeks pass before my eyes: Baby Annabel being dropped. Baby Annabel held upside down as she is fed. Baby Annabel being wrapped tightly in a plastic bag for her part as Baby Moses on the Nile in Charlie's Egypt play.

"The doll is defective," I maintain. "He was just playing with her. He didn't do anything to her eye."— "That I know of" is the part I don't say out loud.

"It's okay," Charlie reassures us. "I don't mind that she has Spooky Eye."

But I can't let it drop, and the next day I decide that I'm going to take her back to the toy store and get a new Baby Annabel. "Exactly the same as the first one," I promise Charlie.

"Okay," he agrees and brings me the doll.

I notice that Baby Annabel now sports black nail polish on her fingernails and toenails as well as in streaks that drip down her hands and wrists.

I sigh.

"I can't take Baby Annabel back to the store if she's covered with nail polish."

"Really, I don't care about the eye," Charlie says again and gives her a cuddle.

I realize that he's grown to love Baby Annabel, Spooky Eye and all. And maybe that is the lesson he will take with him as he grows up—that when you love someone you take the whole package, even the spooky bits.

My son rocks his baby doll gently and her eyes start to close. Her left eye, anyway.

—Jody Mace

Cobbler's Apron

On summer mornings, my mother donned a cobbler's apron with five pockets and took off with the dog to check all the window wells of neighbors' cellars. Her mission? Rabbit rescue.

The Kansas subdivision where we lived had been pasture just a year earlier and the rabbits were still confused. Baby bunnies, looking for a burrow, any burrow, or perhaps just trying to hop from here to there, fell into the window wells. They would have met a dismal fate if it hadn't been for my mother.

Every morning in early summer and continuing for the few weeks it took the bunnies to develop some common sense, Mother tied on a cobbler's apron with five pockets around the bottom edge and set out on her quest. She scooped exhausted, dehydrated, and frightened little bunnies from the eighteen-inch-deep pits and popped them into her pockets. Ginger, our golden retriever, caught on quickly, racing ahead to check all the houses on our block and barking whenever she found a victim.

As the rising sun banished the dewdrops, Mother returned home with her apron pockets overflowing with brown and befuddled furry critters, soft ears and big eyes showing above the pocket tops. More than once, she came into the bedroom where I lay sleeping and unloaded her menagerie onto my bed.

To waken from the sleep of childhood surrounded by a bevy of bunnies was magic. Mother and I played with them for a few hours before releasing them, and I've had a fondness for cobbler's aprons ever since.

Like most women of the fifties, Mother stayed home all day, running the household with the skill of a domestic engineer. She donned her cobbler's apron before she served us breakfast and didn't remove it until right before dinner. Then she put it on again to wash the dishes, tidy up the kitchen, supervise homework, and monitor the evening baths of us kids. She took it off for the last time as we pulled storybooks from the shelves and curled up together to read *Little Women* or *Swiss Family Robinson*.

It seemed to me that the pockets of her apron held enough supplies to support her on a trek across the rolling prairies if necessary. Her standard inventory usually included tissue, dog biscuits, Band-Aids, clothespins, crayons, lipstick, raisins, and rubber bands. Hershey bars and bananas, Mother's interpretation of survival food, often made an appearance, and that apron was always the first place my father looked for the mail and the car keys. It was usually the last place, too.

Her apron achieved mythic status one August afternoon when she was walking us home from the park. We were still two blocks from our house when the jingle-jangle ice cream truck approached, and we looked at my mother wordlessly, dirt-smudged cheeks and pleading eyes speaking volumes, I'm sure. She scrambled into the depths of all five pockets and came up with enough dimes among the plastic barrettes and paperclips and Barbie doll shoes to buy each of us an Eskimo Pie or a Drumstick.

Years have passed since those hot summers in Kansas when I was a child with grass stains on my knees and bunnies in my bed. Now I have children of my own and we live in California. No one seems to wear cobbler's aprons any more. Except for my mother.

My parents moved to California to be closer to us, and we frequently drive into the Sierra foothills to visit them. We went up for a long weekend recently, and on our arrival, my mother greeted us, saying to my youngest son, "I have something for you."

She began searching through the many pockets of her apron. My son's eyes grew wider and wider as she produced a tube of lipstick, a library card, three pens, several paperclips, a plastic spoon, grocery store coupons, and a Hershey bar.

"Whoa! Thanks, Gramma," he said, reaching for the Hershey bar.

"You can have it, but that's not what I was looking for," she said, still searching.

"Oh, Bill," she said to my father, who was watching with a bemused smile, "here's that tiny little screwdriver you were looking for. How on earth did it get in here?"

"I can't imagine why I didn't think to search there in the first place," he said, and she gave him a look.

"Here it is," she announced in triumph, and she pulled out a zipped baggie with some coins inside. "There's a penny, nickel, dime, quarter, fifty-cent piece, and a silver dollar, all from the year you were born."

"Cool, Gramma. Thanks a lot."

He took another bite of the chocolate. "Mom, why don't you have one of these magic aprons?"

My mother pulled on the sash, removed her apron, and, with me still holding my overnight bag in my hand, she tied it around my waist.

"Here, dear. I have plenty of these cobbler aprons. Now you have one, too."

—Peggy Vincent

The Tao of Laundry

My mother imparted many gems of wisdom to me over the years, but perhaps the one that stayed with me the longest had to do with laundry. I was about twelve or thirteen years old when she took me aside one day. I was sure I was finally going to hear the facts of life and was kind of squirming, because I had already gleaned said information eons ago from my two older sisters. It wasn't something I cared to discuss with Mom, for goodness sakes.

Instead, she fixed me with a look of grave significance. "I'm going to need more help around the house now that I've gone back to work," she began, "and I thought you could start by giving me a hand with the laundry."

My sense of relief was palpable. I would have agreed to anything at that point in order to get out of having The Talk, so I simply nodded.

Mom went on to give me a kind of abbreviated version of Laundry 101.

"And you must never ever mix the lights with the darks," she concluded.

There was something about the way she uttered those last words that made me suspect she'd come about that knowledge the hard way. Perhaps, as a child, she put a bright red skirt into a load of her father's white shirts and her mother never forgave her for it. I don't know. Never mixing lights with darks simply became a cardinal rule of doing the laundry that I never challenged.

As the next several years flew by, I became a skilled laundress and even learned to iron so well that Mom stopped sending Dad's shirts out to the ironing lady. At ten cents for a shirt, for two pillowcases, or for three of Dad's starched white handkerchiefs (which a gentleman of that era was never without), I was fairly rolling in the money by the time I headed off to college. At that point, I was also relieved to swap the more arduous task of doing laundry for a family of seven to doing only my own.

This was about the time I first discovered Laundromats. Laundromats seem to come with their own unwritten rules, and I learned early on not to leave laundry unattended in the dryer all afternoon, or you were likely to find your clothes lying out on the folding table for all the world to see. I came from a family that didn't believe in airing its dirty laundry, either literally or figuratively, but I soon discovered that it was almost equally embarrassing to find someone pawing through your clean laundry and fingering your undergarments.

One day I met the man of my dreams, in a computer class of all places, and I knew we were in it for the long haul the first time we did our laundry together. Soon, he popped the question, and the next thing you know, we were married and the proud owners of a new laundry basket. Well, as they say, first comes love, then comes marriage, and a mere eighteen months later, there we were with a new baby in the proverbial baby carriage, which was actually a streamlined stroller.

With sleepless nights now the norm and with the incessant pile of cloth diapers and baby items that needed to be laundered, change was inevitable. That's how we ended up buying our very first home, complete with a washer and dryer. Diamonds may be forever, but a washing machine with a newborn is a daily necessity. That spelled the end of our Laundromat days.

Two more children completed our family, and our washing machine was put to good use on everything from torn and stained blue jeans to lacy dresses.

Thank goodness for the hand-wash cycle. Thanks, also, to permanent press, I all but retired my iron, too. That reminds me of Mom's favorite anecdote, which dates back to a very memorable visit she made when my oldest son was about five or six years old. As the story goes, she asked him where our iron was, as she needed to touch up her clothes, which were wrinkled from being packed in the suitcase.

"And can you imagine?" she always concludes. "He didn't even know what an iron was!"

I, of course, always bristled at that story. Certainly he knew what an iron was! It was that thing we used to melt our fuse beads together.

I'm not actually sure why Mom needed an iron, anyway, though. She has this unique talent to finger press clothes so efficiently as she lovingly folds them that they come out looking like they have been pressed with a real iron. It is one of her many passions in life, and whenever I go to visit her, I always let her do my laundry, even though I feel just a wee bit guilty about it sometimes. Still, I rationalize that I am actually doing her a favor, as it makes her so happy. One time, she spent the entire last morning of my visit drying and folding my clothes.

"But, Mom," I protested, "I'm just going to wash them all again, anyway, when I get home, to get the smell of airplane fuel out of them."

"You're not flying home with dirty clothes," Mom declared firmly.

One look at her determined expression, and I knew it was hopeless to try to convince her otherwise. So she packed my clean and meticulously folded clothes neatly into my suitcase and sent me on my way.

Wouldn't you know that when we went to pick up that suitcase on the other end, there was a suitcase that looked suspiciously similar to it going in the other direction as we approached the carousel.

"Hey, that's our suitcase," my husband exclaimed.

"Not possible," I replied adamantly.

"Have you ever seen another one that even remotely looks like it?" he demanded.

"Well, no," I had to concede.

Our oversize suitcase with the dented corner where a baggage cart had run over it was strictly one of a kind.

We were still debating the issue when our suitcase and the man pulling it disappeared around the corner, never to be seen again, rendering our discussion moot. I just have to hope that, whoever the man was and whatever his reason for walking off with our suitcase, he at least took the time to admire Mom's perfectly beautiful folding job before he deep-sixed the contents. If he was hoping for jewels or electronics, he was going to be sadly disappointed.

While my interest in ironing waned over the years, my laundry skills, especially in the stain-removing area, were on the rise. With two active boys, I felt like a walking commercial for laundry soap and stain removers. It was those football pants that gave me my greatest challenge. Who but a man would have thought white an appropriate color for pants that were to be worn by a bunch of little boys who were tackling each other in the mud?

When I finally found a stain remover that removed not only mud stains but also grass stains, it was too good not to share.

"Can you believe it," I gushed to a friend as we stood on the sidelines cheering on our future NFLers. "I found a product that makes his game pants look almost new, and I only have to run them through the washing machine once, instead of three times—" I broke off, horrified, realizing that for the last five minutes I had been extolling the virtues of my favorite stain remover. I, who was once going to change the world, was now discussing my laundry (dirty or otherwise) in public! *Please, someone stop me*, I thought, *before I start expounding on how my laundry soap makes the whites come out whiter and the brights brighter.*

Time went by, and suddenly, there I was, prepping my oldest child for college. *Have I taught him enough? Will he make the right choices? Does he know how to do his own laundry?*

Solemnly, I took him aside and bequeathed to him the laundry secret that Mom had passed along to me. "Son," I said, "don't forget all we have taught you, make good choices, and always remember to separate the lights from the darks when you do your laundry."

Weeks later, I was awakened in the middle of the night by the shrill insistence of the telephone. My heart pounded in fear as I mentally took inventory of my loved ones. *Are any of my children still out for the night? Could something have happened to my eldest son? To my parents?*

The familiar voice on the other end of the line sounded surprisingly perky. "Mom?" my son said.

I'm not quite sure who he expected to answer the phone at this hour. I struggled to wake up.

"What is it, honey?" I asked frantically. "Is everything okay? Did something happen?"

"Hey, relax, Mom. You know how you always told me not to put lights and darks together in the same load?"

My brain finally snapped awake. I glanced over at the friendly green numbers on my clock radio and groaned. "Honey, let's get this straight: It's three o'clock in the morning and you're calling me to discuss laundry?"

His voice was sheepish. "Uh, sorry, Mom. I didn't know it was so late. I just thought you'd like to know . . ." He broke off.

"Know what?" My mom radar was alert again. Maybe this was something bigger than laundry.

"Oh, well, yeah . . ." he mumbled. Then suddenly, the words came out all in a rush. "Well, I put them all into the same load, together . . ."

"Yes?" The suspense was unbearable.

"And nothing happened."

"Nothing happened?" I echoed dumbly.

After he hung up, I was suddenly wide awake. It may seem like a small thing to most people, but for me this was absolutely momentous. I couldn't have been more stunned if someone had informed me that the man I have been married to all these years was really an alien from another planet. My son had just exploded a carefully guarded laundry secret that had been handed down for over three generations. My mind spun. *If that venerable advice didn't pan out, what else that my parents had told me or that I'd told my children would turn out to be untrue too?*

There was only one thing to do. I called Mom early that morning.

"Mom," I said without any preface, "Were you aware that it's okay to commingle lights with darks?"

I will say this for Mom: nothing fazes her. I can call her at all hours and ask her absolutely anything, giving her no context whatsoever, and she immediately picks up on whatever it is I'm talking about.

"Well, yes, dear," she said brightly, "I've known that for years. With these new fabrics, you don't really have to worry about the colors bleeding anymore."

So, Mom was in on it too. I suddenly felt like the victim of The Great Laundry Sorting Hoax. Here I was, blithely going along, living my life and sorting my dirty clothes into light and dark piles for years, when, all the time, it was unnecessary. Honestly! Why am I always the last to know?

—*Cara Holman*

Penciling It In

Long before I became pregnant, when I wasn't even thinking of it, I went to see a movie with my mother-in-law and Lauren, a womanfriend of mine. At the time, Lauren was the mother of a delightful toddler daughter and was also eight months pregnant.

After the film, Lauren and my mother-in-law were talking about "staying home," and my mother-in-law said, "It's the same thing every day. Pick up this, fold that, put this away. Over and over. But you don't mind it."

Lauren nodded.

At the time, I thought her comment mostly reflected my mother-in-law's peculiar obsessive-compulsive nature—but I also thought that there was truth in it—that being a mother might just be

that repetitive, that mindless, that boring. That

filled with constant cleaning and housework. So I put off getting pregnant for several more years.

As young women, we sometimes feel we have a heavy burden to carry and a hard choice to make. In the past, we are told, most successful women were not mothers. Emily Dickinson and Virginia Woolf come to mind. Hermits and suicidals—these were our role models. So often, young women put off having children in order to focus first on their careers. I waited until I was thirty-two to try to get pregnant; by then, I had received my PhD and published my first book. Order, plans, schedules—these ruled my life, and I wasn't quite sure how motherhood would fit in with that.

When my daughter was a baby, I found myself, just as my mother-in-law predicted, repeating the same activities over and over. Groceries on Monday. Laundry on Tuesday. Vacuum on Thursday. Pick up toys at 8:00 each night after the baby went to bed. I stuck to my plan like a general, as if the life of my army, the foot soldiers in my mind, depended on it. I felt fulfilled, gratified, truly at peace when my house was clean and orderly. I savored my cleaning supplies like perfumes, keeping them locked up in a cabinet and using them sparingly, endowing them with the power to make my life beautiful. I knew this was slightly—crazy. But I couldn't stop.

There is a goddess of order, and it comes as no surprise that she is also a mother. According to Chinese mythology, the mother of all creation is Nu Kua, who first created humans out of clay and then got to work bringing the universe out of chaos by cleaning up. Putting up some pillars to hold up the sky. Decorating the clouds with jewels so rain would come. Straightening the land so crops could be sown. But this is all that is known about her. I look in book after book and can find no further stories about her. There is no plot to her life. She tidied up. Then disappeared. End of story.

My need for order was almost the end of a story in my life.

I have a friend who, though far away, sustains me through her letters. She is also a mother, her boy having been born two weeks before my girl.

Sometimes she goes away. A blackness takes her; she falls into a hole. Or a redness takes her, something I've said. She retreats, and then—after weeks, or months, or, once, a year—she comes back.

One time, when my daughter was a toddler, I had not heard from her in three weeks. Three weeks and three days. Twenty-four days. Almost a month. I'd been counting. The reason, that time, was my need for order. I had asked her if another womanfriend of mine could stay with her overnight on a journey west. My friend said no, her house was a mess. And she had felt such shame and incompetence about this that she fell silent. It took her almost a month to find the courage to tell me this.

I was reading her letter, on the day when it finally arrived, while my toddler daughter, Lily, played nearby, and I had a sudden urge to rush to my stationery, wanting to explain. But I didn't. Lily brought me a book and wanted me to read, sat down in my lap, and so I read.

Hours went by. I made dinner and cleaned up from dinner, and put Lily to bed, and straightened the house, and slept, and woke up, and did the breakfast dishes, and mopped the kitchen floor, and . . .

Suddenly it hit me. *My friend is right. I am— what? obsessed? frenzied? dictatorial? crazy?—about order and cleanliness.*

And it almost pushed my beloved friend completely away from me. This image she had of me, of my house, haunted her and spooked her out of meeting an interesting woman who was on her way to live in an ashram, which would have been wonderful fodder for a character. And it kept her from sharing her feelings with me—all because she feared what the friend would report back to me about the cleanliness of her house.

Many middle-class white women have been brainwashed into becoming Cleaning Police. When we go into each other's homes, we either exclaim, "Oh, how nice!" when we see cleanliness and order, or we stay silent and judge while the other woman apologizes.

I think back to my pre-mothering past. I was in a women's group, and we would meet at each other's houses every other week. Each woman's house was spotless. Beautiful. You could eat off the floors. Literally. One woman vacuumed every day. Every day. She once spent so much money on a new vacuum that she was afraid her husband would be angry, so she kept it in her neighbor's garage and went to get it each day after her husband left for work. This group eventually ended.

As soon as one begins to divide things up, there are names;

Once there are names, one should know when to stop;

Knowing when to stop, one thereby avoids peril.

—Tao Te Ching

I needed to know when to stop. In that letter, my friend had asked me, "How do you work, keep your home clean, write, mother, and be a wife all at once?"

The truth is, I didn't. I did one thing at a time, when I had planned to do it. Gave it all my attention, then left it behind. And this made me, certainly, somewhat rigid. Organized, competent, and clear-headed, yes. But hard, stiff, unyielding.

Womanfriends did not "stop by" my house. Lauren used to, the one with two young children, but I asked her to stop. I didn't like being surprised. My house was a mess. Or I was writing. Busy. My day was planned.

But over the years, as my daughter grew, so did I. And the seeds of my growth could be seen in that moment—when I had the impulse to write to my friend and defend and explain my position, but then Lily asked me to read a book and I took her in my lap and read. This is akin to the Taoist philosophy of Lao Tzu from China, which the West has often misinterpreted as passivity and "doing nothing." Was I really "doing nothing" when I read to my daughter in that moment? There are many people in our culture, men and women alike, who might say yes. But as mothers, we must have the courage to say no.

Our growth as mothers comes from learning to bend and sway with the seasons, to pay attention to what—and who—is right in front of us at the moment. Yes, we plan. Yes, we clean. Yes, we organize. Yes, we pencil things in. But once all that is done, we find ways to leave the arranging behind and to drop deeply into a kind of presence from which all creation and all love comes.

Without exception, every woman I know who mothers and also makes time for a creative passion or a career had to decide at some point in their lives to let the house go. To let go. They relaxed their standards. They stopped trying to be perfect. They learned not to rearrange the dishes in the dishwasher after the husband had already loaded it. They allowed the teenager's room to be a pigsty and got into the habit of shutting the door.

I sometimes wonder about Nu Kua. I wonder if she didn't know when to stop, if there are no stories about her because she cleans, still. Not very much narrative action in that. "And now the drapes are hung. And now the floor is mopped. And now the windows are done."

Or maybe there are no stories about her because she stopped too suddenly. Broke down. Fell apart. Couldn't take it anymore. For many mothers, the legacy of Sylvia Plath's suicide haunts us. The way she put out breakfast for the children before doing it.

Something deep within us nods at this gesture. We know the well of love she felt for them even as the love she felt for herself ran dry.

So much has changed since the only role models we writer women had were Dickinson and Woolf and Plath. The writings of many women of color, women who historically have always had to balance work and family, have given us new pathways to follow. Women scholars such as Paula Feldman and Beverly Guy-Sheftall have unearthed the work of black and white American women from before the twentieth century who were mothers and successful writers at the same time. And the work of contemporary mother writers continues to inspire us in ways our foremothers couldn't have imagined—as we e-mail and blog and Skype and connect through web-based publications like *Literary Mama*.

Other things have changed, as well. My mother-in-law passed away last December, and every time I fold laundry or make a list for groceries or smile at my daughter who carries her name, I miss her. I miss her mothering presence, and I honor her memory by being lovingly present with the task at hand. Over the last few generations of women, we have seen the pendulum swing back and forth between domesticity and career. When I am present and aware enough to appreciate what and who is right in front of me, I think that perhaps we are reaching a middle point, a point of peace with ourselves as mothers.

And peace cannot be penciled in. It must be attended to again and again. Like picking up this. And folding that. And putting the other thing away. But you don't mind it. Because you do it all with love. And love is really the point of it all, at the end of a life or at the end of each day.

—*Cassie Premo Steele*

Some names in the story have been changed to protect the privacy of those individuals and their families.

Walking Our Mothers

Something has switched between us; our roles are reversed; my hand is leading hers. A late summer sun sears our backs, shadows our faces. The meadow crests into nothingness, a clean sweep of hill emblazoned by blue sky. Our feet seek the seam of hard-packed clay between tall grasses going to seed. Our pace finds a rhythm in the rising heat, up the trail to a dusty summit.

My mother's breath softens as a female marsh hawk skims over the abandoned orchard ahead of us. With deep chocolate and taupe feathers, the hawk pivots her head to the right, then to the left, searching for any scurrying vole, field mouse, or exposed songbird. Our legs imitate her sweeping confidence, her owning of this place.

My mother used to be my link to the world beyond the door, my anchor, when I was so little and light that

I felt like I could lift off in a slight breeze. She opened the door for my brother and me to a quiet pond in the northern Michigan woods. Throughout dramatic changes in her life—going back to school, divorce, single motherhood—my mother kept our cabin as a place of refuge, a center point for all our wanderings. We spent summers playing in mucky pond sand and writing our own lore on the pink undersides of birch bark. The dark canopy of white pine and northern spruce hid our "bear dens" and secret places. The pond and the woods were the world where we moved beyond boundaries, from doorstep to cattails, from chores to our imagination. Unless it was raining or time for bed, we could not quiet the day that called to us with its insistent humming.

We followed our mother into meadows of knee-high blueberry bushes before the deer and bears could fill their bellies with the tart, wild fruit. We floated out to meet her on plastic rafts, the water cool to our fingers and toes, out to where she gleamed, oil-covered, in the sun. She showed us how to create rock animals, collages of driftwood, shells, and leaves with the pooling miracle of Elmer's glue. She wove macramé from a low branch at the water's edge, the wind sifting both her hair and the rough ropes in pulses. She crafted owl-shaped wall hangings into shape, catching thick sticks with their knotted talons.

When did it change, when did we cross over? When did I begin to lead her out into fields, into the brightness of the larger world? Was she the mother, the child, or the friend guided out of grief by another? At the summit of the trail now, the boundaries of our roles suddenly blurred as we closed our eyes from the sun, relieved for the moment by a brief, total darkness.

My mother visits Portland in mid-August, deep within our "dog days," which is the most deceptive time to visit. The thought of rain, the memory of it, is as parched as the glaciers graying on the mountains. Her visit this time is short; over the weekend we will attend a sixtieth wedding anniversary party for her best friend's parents. Friends and family are flying in from all over the country, joy at reuniting lifting them above the reality of the bride's ailing health, that this might be their last chance to be with her. In the cloudless sky, their planes approach from the east, brilliant white birds winging their way to land.

It is a necessary trip for my mother, whose own mother died suddenly in May. Since then, she has not stepped back from the daily chore of living, and this trip might give her a chance to catch her breath. As her parents' only child, she makes weekly, four-hour trips to visit her father. Her job as a medical office manager coupled with looking after her husband and their six dogs and cats have taken a visible toll. She is weary, heavy-eyed, and close to tears, especially throughout the anniversary celebration.

At the party we sip wine, refold our linen napkins after the luncheon. We relax into the groom's words of gratitude, how full his life has been because of his wife and their children, grandchildren, and friends. We all become fragile and open in the heat, with the wine, and with his declarations. After the couple kisses for the crowd, clanging on their crystal, my mother excuses herself and leaves the room. I don't follow her.

Motherless, she is finally at a loss, she is lost. She cannot chill her sadness with dismissive busyness. On vacation, there is nothing to do, no one to manage. My mother has never been without her mother, and no one has ever trusted solely in me to figure out the next step.

In the late afternoon, my large, cool house welcomes us back with its thick mahogany doors, crown molding, and leaded windows. We wait out the afternoon as if waiting for a storm to break, the good clearing that comes from thunderclaps and a sharp, summer rain. I have washed and spread out new, striped sheets on the futon, tucking in all the corners the way my nurse-mother taught me. Fluffed and stacked pillows promise her a dark and dream-less sleep.

My mother and I fall into an easy routine when-ever she visits—the parading of new clothes, full photo albums, and gifts from her deep leather bag. We continue this way, unfolding, dropping the day around us like new, tight shoes. Open windows let the evening air sift in, heavy with the scent of black-berries ripening along the street. A moth invites itself in and heads for the lit candle in a brilliant death wish.

We sip tea, and the night wraps around us like a thin shawl. She lets me break out my tarot deck (a Zen Buddhist deck, not very witchy for a conserva-tive, Lutheran mother) and watches the cards deliver messages for us to decipher. The images are full of lone figures, many of children on cliffs, at gates, on shadowy paths. Each are about to leap off, embark on a strange journey. There is no longer any pre-tense. No one, not even me, can tether her, and she comes loose. She sits on a pile of pillows, low to the ground, where she can finally be grounded, cry, and begin to grieve.

By morning, her face is sheet-stained and pink. I pour her a cup of strong coffee with cream and pull back the curtains. We sit on the porch rocking chairs like a couple of old ladies, watching the birds along the calm, blanched street. Later, I will take her to an appointment with my massage therapist and then to lunch with her best friend. But first, we decide to hike up to the summit of Powell Butte.

We arrive at the gravel parking lot, and the dog leaps out of the car and begins her mouse-pouncing dance. All the mountains are visible with low, hazy clouds circling them like skirts. My mother's Midwestern-trained eyes lift up as I scan the trees and air for any bird crossing or calling. We take a trail up to a wide and wild meadow; from here I have seen fox and kestrels, western meadowlarks and lazuli buntings. Today, purple vetch twines around the tall grasses. Barn swallows nip at the air, chatting with each other past our shoulders. A marsh hawk takes off from her silent fence post and the air suddenly clears, severed by her low soaring.

A rail-tie map at the summit radiates 360 degrees, pointing to the buttes and extinct and active volcanoes etched below: Mt. Hood, Mt. St. Helens, Silverstar, Mt. Adams, Rocky Butte, the West Hills, Mt. Jefferson, and Jenne Butte. An old pear orchard leans silver, yet heavy with fruit, in the nearly silent morning. The lightness that surrounds us contrasts with the night before; it lends clarity about what is best to do for my mother, the flailing child. Beyond carefully mapped streets and their funneled traffic, the curve of the land is uncemented and alive. Our walking feels like a meditation into something fuller than this ordinary day. We can love ourselves, our situations and losses, and the land by following a thin vein of trails and accepting the given, imperfect views. In following these corridors deep into our hearts, we can learn to transform our pain into another way of being, into a new identity. From child to mother, from mother to crone. There is no promise of arrival, only an unending ramble.

We grow warm under our layers, and by the time we get back to the car, we are thirsty and hungry. The day's schedule waits. My mother will receive her first full-body massage, will walk down the crowded sidewalk like a woman floating. My hand will let go as she finds her own way past the bookstores, flower vendors, and musicians. She will be suspended above her grief, even for such a small moment. Buoyed by her first solo flight, she will be confident that there is someone below waiting for her when she lands.

—*Kristin Berger*

This story was first published in LiteraryMama.com.

Contributors

Linda Avery ("An Ordinary Day") lives along the shore of Lake Michigan with her husband and two golden retrievers. She has two grown children who constantly keep alive the laughter in her life. She credits her husband and her amazing writing mentor and friend for inspiring her to write her stories.

Katherine Barrett ("Heart Stories") is a Canadian writer living in South Africa with her husband and three preschoolers. Her thoughts on motherhood have been published in *Cahoots Magazine*; *Mom Writer's Literary Magazine*; the award-winning anthology, *Call Me Okaasan: Adventures in Multicultural Mothering*; and on her blog, twinutero.org.

Joan McClure Beck ("Keeper of the Sash") lives in South Carolina, where she is an adjunct instructor in the transitional studies department of Spartanburg Community College. She has participated in numerous writers' workshops and conferences, and in 2005, she was honored as the Florida Christian Writers' Conference "Writer of the Year." Her publishing credits include stories in *Pockets Magazine*, *God's Handprints*, and anthologies.

Kristin Berger ("Walking Our Mothers") lives with her family in Portland, Oregon, where she serves as an editorial member of VoiceCatcher. She is the author of a poetry chapbook, *For the Willing*, an Oregon Book Award nominee. Her nonfiction has been nominated for the Pushcart Prize.

Mauverneen Blevins ("Empty Nest Christmas"), the mother of three lovely, grown daughters, is enjoying retirement by pursuing her interests in writing and photography. Her work has appeared in several publications, including *A Cup of Comfort® for Christmas*. She currently lives in Reno, Nevada, where she has a new pair of Christmas stockings.

Beverly Burmeier ("Growing Wise") is a freelance writer based in Austin, Texas. She writes about whatever piques her interest, including health, nutrition, travel, family, and gardening, as well as essays and profiles. Her articles have appeared in *Redbook*, *Better Homes and Gardens*, *Glamour*, *American Profile*, and other national and regional publications.

Bobbi Carducci ("Payback") lives in Round Hill, Virginia, with her wonderful husband, Michael. She is currently writing a creative nonfiction book, sharing her sometimes stressful, occasionally very funny, always challenging real-life experiences as an in-home caregiver for her elderly father-in-law. She is a columnist for About Families Publications and a teen writing coach.

Ryan Chin ("Stir-Fry Love") lives in Portland, Oregon, with his wife, three cats, and a dog. He gave up his career as a teacher so he could have the freedom to create. Whether it's short films or writing, the sharing of stories is his passion.

Linda Clare ("Diving In") is the award-winning author of *The Fence My Father Built*, a contemporary novel. The coauthor of three nonfiction books, she teaches novel, essay, and memoir writing at Lane Community College. Linda lives in Eugene, Oregon, with her husband, Brad, and their five wayward cats.

Julie Crea ("Learning to Fish") is a media editor, freelance writer, and mom from Erie, Colorado. You can find her essays in *A Cup of Comfort*® *for Teachers* (under the name Julie Dunbar), *A Woman's Europe*, and other anthologies. Her work has also been performed on stage and featured on the web journal Admit Two.

Karen Dempsey ("Here Beside Me") lives in Cambridge, Massachusetts, with her family. Her essays have appeared in *Brain, Child* magazine; *Babble*; LiteraryMama.com; and the *Buffalo News*. She is writing a memoir about caring for an infant with chronic medical needs.

Cathy Crenshaw Doheny ("A Whisper") is an award-winning freelance writer specializing in creative nonfiction. Her pieces have been featured in various online and print publications. She currently writes for examiner.com as the international adoption examiner, the organ and tissue donor examiner, and the blood cancers examiner. Cathy lives in Charlotte, North Carolina, with her husband, Kevin, and their daughter, Jade.

Connie Ellison ("My Mother's Hands") is the author of the book *Any Road: The Story of a Virginia Tobacco Farm*. She is married to Andrew

Ellison and has two children, Jean Prince and James Moses. She teaches English at Sandusky Middle School in Lynchburg, Virginia.

Elizabeth King Gerlach ("Just a Mom") is the mother and stepmother of Nick, Ben, Michael, and James. She lives in Oregon with her husband, Scott. She has written two books on autism, *Just This Side of Normal: Glimpses into Life with Autism* and *Autism Treatment Guide*, and several of her stories have been published in the *Cup of Comfort®* series.

Kim Girard ("One Fat Frog and the Tyranny of Toys") is a freelance journalist whose work has appeared in publications such as the *San Francisco Chronicle Magazine*, *Fast Company*, CNET, and *Slow Trains Literary Journal*. She lives in Brookline, Massachusetts, with her husband and daughter. She just finished writing her first children's book.

Tessa Graham ("The Tiring, Exhausting, Patience-Testing, Very Long Day") works for the British Columbia provincial government, but in August 2009, she took a year off and moved with her family to a small village in the south of France to have a new family adventure! Andrew and Charlotte are now thirteen and eleven and still don't relate to Alexander and his terrible, horrible, no good, very bad day.

Andrea Harris ("The Mominator") is the mother of William and Joshua and the daughter of Lorna and Andrew. She teaches women's studies and English composition at Wright State University in Dayton, Ohio. Her published writing includes pieces on children with autism, single mothers, and violence against women.

Cara Holman ("The Tao of Laundry") lives in Portland, Oregon, with her husband and the youngest of their three children. A former computer programmer/systems analyst, she now proudly calls herself a "mom writer." Her personal essays, creative nonfiction, and poetry have appeared in print, in various online journals, and on her blog, Prose Posies.

Cathy Howard ("Sister Rita Maureen and Mom") teaches English at Central Catholic High School in Grand Island, Nebraska, where her husband, John, also teaches. They have two sons, Kenny and Tommy, and two cats, Willy and Blackie. In 2008, Cathy completed a book with her ten brothers and sisters, titled *Our House*, and contributed a story to *A Cup of Comfort® for Breast Cancer Survivors*.

Jennifer A. Howard ("Fair Division") lives in Marquette, Michigan, where she teaches English at Northern Michigan University.

Sally Jadlow ("Thanksgiving at Jennifer's") teaches writing in the Kansas City area. She also serves as a chaplain to corporations. She is the author of *The Late Sooner*, an historical novel, as well as poetry and short stories. Four children, twelve grandchildren, and a husband fill her life.

Amy Lou Jenkins ("Three P.M.) writes from Wisconsin, where she lives with her husband, son, and two mutts. Her first book, *Every Natural Fact: Five Seasons of Open-Air Parenting*, will be released in June 2010 by HolyCow! Press, and she is widely published in creative nonfiction periodicals and anthologies. She teaches writing at workshops, seminars, and local universities.

Melinda Jensen ("The Company of Angels") lives in Toowoomba, Australia, where she works part-time in the mental health sector. Her daughters and grandchildren provide plenty of fodder for her children's stories and for the two novels she is currently crafting. A number of her short stories, poems, and articles have appeared in national and international publications.

Ramona John ("True North") was judge of a juvenile court. Now retired, she lives in Texas with her husband, Dick, and their dogs, matronly German Shepherd Greta and rescue dog Jake, the mutt who makes them smile. Her published works include two books, magazine and newspaper articles, and stories in several anthologies, including several *Cup of Comfort®* volumes.

Kimila Kay ("Hates Kids") balances her love of writing with meeting the needs of her investment-company clients. She lives with her husband, Randy, and Boston terrier, Maggie, in Portland. Her essays also appear in *A Cup of Comfort® for Single Mothers* and *A Cup of Comfort® for the Grieving Heart*.

Jolie Kanat ("A Nonstandard Mother") is a professional writer in every medium, including a nonfiction book, *Bittersweet Baby*; a column for the *San Francisco Chronicle*; essays for NPR radio's Perspectives; songs for Time Warner and Universal Studio productions; and greeting cards for Schurmann Fine Papers. She has also produced two CDs for children with special needs.

Elizabeth Klanac ("Missing . . . You") lives in North Ridgeville, Ohio, with her cat, Ginger, and works as a printer. Her son, Kevin, a National Merit scholar, attends Ohio State University. Elizabeth also has an essay in *A Cup of Comfort® for Single Mothers*.

Tina Lincer ("Dance Lessons") has written about motherhood, work, and dance for the *Albany Times Union*, *Los Angeles Times Syndicate*, *Chicago Sun-Times*, *Writer's Digest*, and *The Women's Times*. Her essays also have been featured on public radio and in the *A Cup of Comfort®* series and other anthologies. A writer for Union College, she lives in upstate New York.

Nikki Loftin ("The Best Days of Our Lives") is an award-winning freelance writer, former teacher, and family ministry director. She lives, writes, and cooks near Austin, Texas, with her Scottish husband, two rowdy sons, two dogs, and five chickens.

Glenys Loewen-Thomas ("Look Out, Wonder Woman!") lives in Salem, Oregon, with her husband and five children. She divides her time between parenting, teaching college writing and literature, and writing short stories and essays. She is currently working on her memoir, a comical look at life as a disorganized, overtaxed mother, the pressure to do everything, and the sometimes toxic mix of the two.

Shawn Lutz ("Uh-Oh, Here Comes the Cheerio Mom!") lives in beautiful Capistrano Beach, California, with her wonderful husband and their two spectacular children. She enjoys full-time motherhood with some part-time writing, singing, sewing, and cooking. This is her fourth publication in the *A Cup of Comfort®* book series.

Jody Mace ("A Change in the Wind" and "Love Blind") is a writer in Charlotte, North Carolina, who has written for O magazine, *Parents*, and the *Washington Post*. She also blogs on her website, CharlotteOnTheCheap.com.

Tricia L. McDonald ("Butterfly") is a published writer/editor and the owner/operator of A Writing Passage: Where Stories Are Created. Often referred to as a "manuscript midwife," Tricia teaches creative writing classes and offers manuscript editing and one-on-one writing assistance. She resides in Grand Haven, Michigan.

Melanie Springer Mock ("On Sons, at Four") is the mother of two boys and an associate professor of writing and literature at George Fox University. Her essays have appeared in *Christian Feminism Today*, LiteraryMama.com, and *The Chronicle of Higher Education*, among other places. Her book, *Writing Peace*, was published by Cascadia in 2003.

Paula Munier ("In Search of the Perfect Meringue") is a veteran writer and editor who has yet to master the art of meringue—or to marry Pergola Man. But she's working on it. She lives in a little lakeside cottage in the great Commonwealth of Massachusetts with her family and two dogs. Her pet memoir, *Fixing Freddie*, will be published by Adams Media in 2010.

Jean Knight Pace ("Rings") has had work published in journals ranging from *Puerto del Sol* to the *Dollar Stretcher* and is a former editor for *Organize* magazine. She lives in southern Indiana with her husband and four children.

Faith Paulsen ("Quick Bright Thing") lives in Norristown, Pennsylvania, with her family. Her work has appeared in *A Cup of Comfort® for Parents of Children with Special Needs*, LiteraryMama.com, and *Wild River Review*, and she was a finalist in Glimmer Train's Short Story Contest for New Writers. She blogs on Open Salon.

Rosalie Sanara Petrouske ("When Autumn Comes") received her MA in English from Northern Michigan University in Marquette, Michigan. She currently teaches writing classes at Lansing Community College in

Lansing, Michigan. Her essays have appeared in *American Nature Writing*, and she has published a chapbook of poetry, *A Postcard from My Mother*. She spends summers with her daughter, Senara, hiking, camping, and teaching her the poetry of the natural world.

Mary C. M. Phillips ("Tiaras and Rhinestones") is a musician and writer of poetry and short stories. She has toured nationally as a keyboardist, bass player, and singer for various rock groups and musical comedy artists. She resides in New York with her husband and son.

Amy Simon ("It Never Ends") is a producer and the writer/performer of Cheerios In My Underwear, the longest-running solo show in Los Angeles, where she lives with her two daughters. She also produces and hosts Motherhood Unplugged, a benefit stage show and radio series. A frequent guest on Air America radio, she writes "Fun Fabulous Female Facts" for The Museum of Motherhood, and her work appears in various publications, such as *LA Parent*, *The Mom Egg*, Shewrites.com, and Mamazine.com.

Heather K. Smith ("Why Today Is Jammie Day") lives in Dublin, Ohio, with her husband, Steve. She has three children, Hope, Liam, and Camryn. Heather has a bachelor's degree from Purdue University and a master's degree from The Ohio State University, but she learns most of what she needs to know from her children.

Cristina Olivetti Spencer ("Crazy Gifts") lives in Palo Alto, California, with her husband and children. She writes between drop-offs and pick-ups at kindergarten and preschool. At the time this essay was written, she was pregnant with her third daughter.

Diane Stark ("Top Ten Reasons I Love Being a Mom") is a former elementary school teacher turned stay-at-home mom and freelance writer. Her work has been published in national publications such as *New Parent*, *MomSense*, and *Woman's World*. Her first book, *Teacher's Devotions to Go*, is due out this fall. She lives in southern Indiana with her husband, Eric, and their five children.

Cassie Premo Steele ("Penciling It In") is the author of five books and hundreds of essays, stories, and poems about mothering and creativity. Her current writing projects include "Birthing the Mother Writer," a column at LiteraryMama.com, and a book based on her workshops and classes on "co-creating." She lives in Columbia, South Carolina.

Peggy Vincent ("Cobbler's Apron"), author of the memoir *Baby Catcher: Chronicles of a Modern Midwife*, has delivered more than 3,000 babies in and around Berkeley, California. Now retired, she lives in Oakland with Roger, her husband of fifty-four years, and their two cats.

Cynthia Washam ("Dear God, Don't Let Me Laugh") is a full-time freelance writer who lives in South Florida with her husband and teenage son. Her droll observations on family life have appeared in more than a dozen newspapers and magazines and the book *A Cup of Comfort® for Mothers to Be*.

Stefanie Wass ("A Few Days Off" and "Just to Be with You") lives in Hudson, Ohio, with her husband and two daughters. A freelance writer, she has published essays in the *Los Angeles Times*, *Seattle Times*, *Christian Science Monitor*, *Akron Beacon Journal*, *Akron Life and Leisure*, *Cleveland Magazine*, and numerous anthologies.

Jamie Wojcik ("My Mother, Myself") is a stay-at-home mom who lives in Hudson, Wisconsin, with her husband and two children. In her spare time, she enjoys knitting, blogging, reading, gardening, and cheering on the Green Bay Packers. She writes about her crazy life as a mom to two young children in her blog Knitting and Mayhem.

About the Editor

Colleen Sell has compiled and edited thirty-three *A Cup of Comfort®* anthologies. She has authored, ghostwritten, or edited more than 100 books, served as editor-in-chief of two award-winning magazines, and been published in numerous periodicals. She and her husband, T. N. Trudeau, live in a turn-of-the-century farmhouse on a forty-acre pioneer homestead in the Pacific Northwest—a two-hour drive from her amazing mother.